Mohandas K. Gandhi
The Last Eighteen Years

A Nonviolence and Social Change Source Book

Mohandas K. Gandhi
The Last Eighteen Years

A Nonviolence and Social Change Source Book

Edited by
Sterling P. Olmsted, Mike Heller, and Ruth Olmsted

Wilmington College Peace Resource Center

Edited by:
Sterling P. Olmsted, Mike Heller, and Ruth Olmsted

Cover photo copyright by:
Caitlin Fitzsimmons, photographer
www.caitlinfitzsimmons.com

Design by:
Mary Ann Mayers
www.Extraordinary Lives.com

Published by:
Wilmington College Peace Resource Center
1870 Quaker Way
Pyle Center Box 1183
Wilmington, OH 45177

ISBN-13: 978-0-9658866-4-2

Acknowledgements

Our thanks to our friends who encouraged us in editing this volume. For help with questions and research, we thank Meeta Mehrotra, Narendra Behari Mehrotra, Anil Shende, Hany Hosny, and Srikanth Mallavarapu. We received and appreciate research help from Usha Thakkar and the staff of the Mani Bhavan Gandhi Sangrahalaya in Mumbai, and from Wendy Chmielewski and the staff of the Swarthmore College Peace Collection. We thank the Virginia Foundation of Independent Colleges for a Mednick Fellowship Grant that supported travel to do research. Our thanks to Katherine Hoffman, Channing Johnson, and colleagues at Roanoke College, and to Roanoke College for grants in time and funding to support this work. For invaluable extended loans of the print version of Gandhi's complete works, we thank Union College in Schenectady, New York and Wilmington College. We especially appreciate the caring support for this publication from James Boland, Director of the Peace Resource Center, Wilmington College; Neil Snarr, Professor Emeritus, Wilmington College; and Daniel A. DiBiasio, President of Wilmington College. We thank Caitlin Fitzsimmons for her wonderful photograph, "Gandhi in San Francisco," of which a detail is used on the front cover, and we thank Mary Ann Mayers and Extraordinary Lives for excellent editing and book design.

We could not have completed this book without the loving support of our spouses—Barbara Olmsted (now deceased), Rebecca Heller, and Larry Syzdek.

Contents

Preface

This volume is different from other collections of Mohandas K. Gandhi's writings in that it is intended to complement Gandhi's *Autobiography: The Story of My Experiments with Truth,* which was published in stages during the 1920s. This book attempts to present Gandhi's life beginning with the Salt March in 1930, his most well-known and successful nonviolent civil disobedience campaign, and ending with his last writings before his assassination in 1948, drawing chiefly on selections from his own writings, but also occasionally on writings of associates, personal friends, and opponents, to enable readers to understand Gandhi's later years—in other words, to finish the Gandhi story. It is a complex story coinciding with the Great Depression, revolutions in various parts of the world, the Spanish Civil War, the rise of Hitler and the formation of the Axis, World War II, and the division of India and Pakistan.

A compilation of this kind, however, cannot ever have the unity of either the *Autobiography* or *Satyagraha in South Africa.* Gandhi did not write an additional volume in the series. Many readers today do not know his record in the political realm. Yet his later newspaper and journal articles, diaries, editorial statements, letters, and speeches, which were published in periodicals such as his own newspaper *Harijan* and later in the *Collected Works of Mahatma Gandhi,* are so voluminous that we had to be selective. We chose what is included here to illustrate how Gandhi continued his "experiments with Truth"—the phrase he used as his *Autobiography's* subtitle. He explains in its introduction, "... it is not my purpose to attempt a real autobiography. I simply want to tell the story of my numerous experiments with truth, ... as my life consists of nothing but those experiments ..." (vii-viii). As he says in the same passage, to write an autobiography is to undertake "a practice peculiar to the West"; instead, he wanted to represent his life as a series of experimental attempts to see what he could accomplish, guided by his sense of spiritual truth. This idea of experimentation resonated with our own ideas of living one's faith. We found in the writings that Gandhi had an amazing range of concerns, and that he kept returning to and refining a comprehensive vision for overcoming the world's problems. We decided to highlight his writings on nonviolence, religion, and economics. These were the major themes of his life's work, and together encompassed interests as wide ranging as economic reform, nonviolent noncooperation, satyagraha, swaraj, Hindu-Muslim unity, eradication of oppressive treatment of untouchables, and the experience of God and faith. The selections show us more clearly who Gandhi was and what he accomplished. We believe it is urgent that students of nonviolence today see Gandhi in action.

More than ten years ago, the editors of this book began planning a series of source books on nonviolence and social change, primarily for college classes but also for the general reader. The first book was on the 18th century Quaker, John Woolman (1720–1772). The second was to be on Mohandas K. Gandhi, but we envisioned several others, and hoped we could enlist editors who would work on other nonviolent change agents, such as Lucretia Mott, Dorothy Day, Abdul Ghaffar Khan, Bayard Rustin, Martin Luther King, and Jeanette Rankin. The project was an ambitious one, and the volume you hold is only the second in the series.

The editors of this volume are Quakers, as was John Woolman. We felt confident that our background gave us some authority as we worked with Woolman's writings. Quaker understanding of nonviolence, peacemaking, and the sacred life in all people helped us to feel a strong connection with Gandhi. But Gandhi was a Hindu whose last words as he was dying from an assassin's bullets were "Raam, Raa … m," calling on his god. What could we bring, if anything, as Quakers to the study of a Hindu? We were encouraged, however, by the fact that Gandhi in the last eighteen years of his life had strong connections with Friends. Reginald Reynolds, a young British Friend, who would later write a book on Woolman, lived in Gandhi's ashram,[1] and Gandhi chose him to carry his Salt March letter to Lord Irwin, explaining what he proposed to do. Later, at the time of the Second Round Table Conference, the important but unsuccessful 1931 negotiations in London to which Gandhi was called, he was hosted and aided by British Friends. He was driven from Folkestone to Friends House in London by Laurence Housman, a Quaker, and welcomed by a largely Quaker reception committee. He visited Woodbrooke, a Quaker educational institution at Selly Oak in Birmingham. It was largely through Friends that his trip to Lancashire was arranged for the purpose of visiting with textile mill workers (Hunt 203),

1. ashram: a retreat or center for communal living, research and study, for followers of a particular path.

and it was in the north of England that he saw Pendle Hill, the place where George Fox, the founder of Quakerism, had his vision of a "great people to be gathered."

One of Gandhi's aides in the later years of his life was Horace Alexander, a British Friend, who was with Gandhi in Calcutta after the war when he succeeded in ending Hindu-Muslim violence in that city. It has been thought that Alexander introduced Gandhi to Woolman's writings, although the evidence for this is sketchy. Also, George Bernard Shaw and MP J. F. Horrabin, with whom Gandhi met while in London for the Round Table Conference, were both members of the socialist Fabian Society, which in 1897 printed 10,000 copies of Woolman's essay "A Plea for the Poor" (Moulton introduction, Woolman 14).

Later, Gandhi began attending New Delhi Friends Meeting, and he tried, though with very little success, to introduce silence into his own ashram prayer meetings. Gandhi would likely have resonated with many of Woolman's ideas about equality, peace, and simplicity. Woolman wrote in his first essay on slavery, published in 1754, "To consider mankind otherwise than brethren, to think favours are peculiar to one nation and exclude others, plainly supposes a darkness in the understanding. For as God's love is universal, so where the mind is sufficiently influenced by it, it begets a likeness of itself and the heart is enlarged towards all men" (202). Woolman wrote in "A Plea for the Poor," probably written in 1763 but first published 1793, "May we look upon our treasures and the furniture of our houses and the garments in which we array ourselves and try whether the seeds of war have any nourishment in these our possessions or not" (255). None of this, of course, is meant to imply a stronger connection with Quakerism than is warranted, but rather to acknowledge our own bias and background, and to explain an affinity we feel for Gandhi's expressions of equality and a Hindu universalism, nonviolence and peace, and opposition to materialism and consumerism in favor of simplicity.

A word about editing: To decrease the burden of in-text citations, we have keyed all of the selections by date and primary source in a Citations listing at the end of the volume. Dates are given at the beginning of selections, and for consistency where there was a choice of dates, such as when a letter was written or a speech delivered and when it was published, the earlier date is given. Approximate dates are indicated by brackets. We have included a Chronology to help provide a context for the writings and a Glossary of terms that will be unfamiliar to many readers. In footnotes, the first occurrence of these terms is also explained, and we identify individuals where possible and where we believe these will be helpful. Punctuation is retained as in the sources, but we have corrected obvious misspellings, which may have been introduced by editors working with Gandhi's writings. References to *CWMG-CD* refer to the CD version of the *Collected Works of Mahatma Gandhi.*

Background for the Study of Gandhi's Life and World

It is presumptuous and perhaps impossible to try to summarize Mohandas K. Gandhi's life and the events of his world in a few pages. What we can do, however, is to provide a brief narrative account and a chronology, with some commentary, as an introduction to the last eighteen years of Gandhi's life.

Mohandas K. Gandhi was born in Gujarat in 1869. His father was Prime Minister of Porbandar, a political entity in Gujarat, serving under British rule. The family followed Indian customs. His mother was an observant Hindu who went to temple and took vows.

Mohan, as Gandhi was called, was married at thirteen to Kastur Makanji Kapadia, who was a few months older (she is later called Kasturba or Kasturbai, meaning with affection "Kastur-mother"). Early in their marriage, they lived mostly with Mohan's parents. Their first child died soon after birth. In 1885 Gandhi's father died, the family fortunes began to decline, and they began looking to Mohan as one who might restore the family. He enrolled in college, but dropped out at the end of the first term. Some advisors suggested that he go to law school in England. Mohan liked the idea, but his family was divided. In 1888 a son, Harilal, was born, and in the same year Mohan sailed for England to study law. The courses were very easy, and Mohan had no difficulty in passing the exams and being admitted to the bar. His mother had insisted on his taking an oath to eat no meat, drink no alcoholic beverages, and avoid sex. Mohan kept his vows, but he put on western clothes and entered the British culture. He learned a great deal in England. He began to think more deeply about religion and culture, and to gain confidence in contrasting his own experiences with what he observed. He also visited France and saw the Eiffel Tower. But he made vegetarianism his principal cause, and had important early experiences, becoming an officer in the London Vegetarian Society and writing articles for *The Vegetarian*.

Mohan returned to India in 1891, where he learned for the first time that his mother had died. He also found that he was not really prepared for the practice of law. He couldn't even examine a witness. His future was not very bright. And in 1892 a second son, Manilal, was born. But in 1893 Mohan accepted an offer of a job for a year in South Africa working for a Muslim merchant who was engaged in a legal struggle with another Muslim merchant. Mohan succeeded in working out a compromise, but also became acutely aware, from his own experience, of racial discrimination and the political oppression of Indians in South Africa. He discovered his own sense of duty to fight against discrimination and for racial equality. He stayed in South Africa, where he took up the cause of Indians of all religions and castes against their white oppressors. And he would eventually bring his family—at that time consisting of Kasturba and four sons (Ramdas would be born in 1897 and Devadas in 1900)—to live in South Africa.

In South Africa Gandhi developed a political strategy that he called satyagraha[2] and employed it in three campaigns. This strategy involved nonviolent resistance and self-suffering. It also involved setting up self-reliant communities, Phoenix Settlement in 1904, and Tolstoy Farm in 1910, and establishing a newspaper, *Indian Opinion*, in 1903. He wrote his first book, *Hind Swaraj,* in 1909, on the dangers of India adopting the harmful practices of Western civilization, also setting out in the book his ideas for India's economic independence. The first campaign of non-violent resistance occurred in 1906 and these continued through 1913. All Gandhi's campaigns employed marches, self-suffering, and the acceptance of imprisonment, and all the while he continued to refine his ideas of satyagraha.

By 1914, Gandhi had become known as a resister to all forms of oppression. He believed that his work in South Africa had been completed, and sailed for India by way of England, arriving in England two days after the outbreak of the First World War. Gandhi, who had organized two nonviolent relief programs in South Africa and served as a nurse in the Boer War and in the Zulu Rebellion, and saw himself as a loyal citizen of the British Empire, promptly offered to set up a similar operation in Europe. But he found himself tangled in red tape, and his health began suffering from the London climate, so in December, after some twenty years working in South Africa, he set sail for India, where he received a hero's welcome in Bombay.

His political mentor, G.K. Gokhale, who had visited him in South Africa, had advised him to spend a year travelling third class in India before taking any kind of political action. Gokhale was now very ill, but Gandhi accepted his advice and spent some time touring India by third-class rail car.

---

2. satyagraha*:* literally, firmness for the truth; truth-force, usually translated as "nonviolent resistance"; the technique developed by Gandhi for social and political change, based on truth, nonviolence, and self-suffering

In Ahmedabad, he established his first Indian ashram, called Satyagraha, and then a larger and more suitable ashram, called Sabarmati, with very strict rules. As Rajmohan Gandhi explains in his monumental biography of his grandfather, "To most Indians an ashram was a selfless and usually religious retreat. By calling his base an ashram Gandhi revealed twin goals, making politics selfless and religion just" (181). Gandhi used the traditional name "ashram" to communicate the religious foundation that he intended to build upon. Not long after returning to India, he was called upon to help the oppressed peasant farmers in Champaran, in the province of Bihar, and in response he organized and carried out the first of his major Indian satyagraha campaigns, solidifying his national heroic status.

There had been hints from the British that after World War I, reforms were necessary and India would be granted Dominion status. With the end of the war in 1918, however, the political situation changed. In Britain the Conservatives assumed control, and the cooperation between Muslims and Hindus, both domestically and internationally, declined with the defeat of the Turks who had supported the Allies. In February 1919, two anti-sedition Rowlatt Bills[3] were introduced, authorizing arrest without trial of Indians suspected of sedition, distributing seditious leaflets, or attending seditious public meetings. Gandhi and other leaders saw in the bills great disrespect and contempt for the Indian people. He convened a meeting in which he and other leaders signed a pledge that they would refuse to obey the laws. As Rajmohan Gandhi writes, "For the first time since 1857, prominent Indians had publicly proclaimed their defiance of British laws" (206). In April 1919, during what Gandhi called "That Memorable Week," Hindus and Muslims joined in a hartal,[4] a nonviolent demonstration, which alarmed British authorities. On April 13, at a peaceful Indian celebration in Amritsar, nearly 400 civilians were slaughtered and over 1,000 wounded by

3. The Rowlatt Bills were named for the judge who headed the commission that recommended them: "The Bills authorized arrests without trial and trials without appeal for suspected seditionists and a two-year sentence for an Indian with a seditious leaflet in his pocket" (Rajmohan Gandhi 205-6).

4. hartal: closing of shops and suspension of work, often as a sign of mourning

troops under General Reginald Dyer,[5] and British-Indian relations changed forever. Another result of the repression was that the government suspended publication of *The Bombay Chronicle*. The two men directing the management of that paper asked Gandhi to take up editorship of two Indian weekly periodicals, *Navajivan* (in Gujarati) and *Young India* (in English), a request that he accepted.

Gandhi felt the British government had betrayed specific promises and commitments. In 1920–21, he launched the first all-India non-cooperation campaign. The British government responded with brutality, there was some violence on the part of Indians, and Gandhi realized that the mass of Indians were not ready for the nationwide satyagraha that he had envisioned. In 1922, in what has been called "the Great Trial," Gandhi was tried for sedition and imprisoned in Yeravda. While in prison, remarkably, he took the opportunity to get his own liberal education. He read some 150 books in several languages. His sentence was for six years, but the state of his health (he had an appendectomy in prison) led to his release in 1924. Off and on throughout the 1920s he worked on writing his *Autobiography*. The first volume was published in 1927, the second in 1929. He also wrote *Satyagraha in South Africa*, which was published in 1928 and gives an account of the South Africa experiences, and, according to Robert Payne, attempts to "redress the balance" of the *Autobiography's* portrayal of himself as hero (377), by making the self less the center of the story. Gandhi used his time during the decade of the 1920s to rethink his approach to Indian independence, while he continued to prepare the Indian people.

In 1930 commenced what we are calling Gandhi's last stage, beginning politically with India's declaration of independence, followed by the dramatic and brilliant nonviolent protest known as the Salt March.

---

5. Besides the massacre, Brigadier Reginald Dyer (1864–1927) had given orders for Indians to crawl in the presence of the British and for the flogging of Indians. He justified his actions as needed to prevent rebellion. He was relieved of his command. After returning to England, he received praise as well as condemnation. (*Historical Dictionary of India*). Sir Michael O'Dwyer (1864–1940), Lieutenant Governor of the Punjab, initially supported General Dyer's repressive measures, and as an opponent of reforms became known "as the most hated man in India." In 1940, O'Dwyer was assassinated in London by a Punjabi Sikh in retaliation for the Amritsar massacre (www.sikhtimes.com).

Gandhi Chronology and Context of Events[6]

1869 Mohandas Karamchand Gandhi born in Porbandar

1882 Marries Kastur Makanji Kapadia

1885 Father dies; first son is born and dies

1887 Gandhi goes to Samaldas College but leaves after first term

1888 Son Harilal born; Gandhi leaves for England to study law; admitted to the Inner Temple

1889–90 Gandhi in England discovers religions; meets Madame Blavatsky and Annie Besant; joins London Vegetarian Society

1891 Gandhi is called to the Bar; returns to India; learns that his mother has died

1892 Fails to establish a successful law practice; son Manilal born

1893 Gandhi leaves India for legal work for an Indian Muslim trading firm in Durban, South Africa

1894 In South Africa founds Natal Indian Congress

1896 Returns to India; publicizes conditions in South Africa in what became known as "The Green Pamphlet" as well as through newspapers and speaking engagements; brings his family back to South Africa, and upon arriving in Durban, he is attacked by a mob stirred to anger by those upset by the way Gandhi had portrayed South Africa

6. Sources for this Chronology include David Cortright's *Gandhi and Beyond*; Rajmohan Gandhi's *Gandhi: The Man, His People, and the Empire*; and Robert Payne's *The Life and Death of Mahatma Gandhi*.

1897 Son Ramdas born

1899–1902 Boer War in South Africa; Gandhi organizes ambulance corps

1900 Son Devadas born

1901–02 Queen Victoria dies; Edward VII becomes king; Gandhi returns to India for a year, where he establishes a successful law practice; then returns to South Africa

1903 Opens law office in Johannesburg; begins publishing the weekly journal *Indian Opinion*

1904 Reads Ruskin's *Unto this Last;* founds the experimental Phoenix Settlement outside Durban

1906 Gandhi makes a vow of celibacy; organizes ambulance corps during Zulu Rebellion; mass meeting of Indians at Empire Theatre in Johannesburg; calls for withdrawal of anti-Asian bills; sails to England to meet with British officials

1907–08 Mass meeting at Johannesburg; general strike; the term "satyagraha" adopted; mass burning of registration certificates; Gandhi's first imprisonment

1909 Gandhi sails to England and on return journey writes *Hind Swaraj*

1910 Edward VII dies; George V becomes king; Japan seizes Korea; *Hind Swaraj* published; Gandhi accepts Hermann Kallenbach's offer of land and founds Tolstoy Farm

1911 Chinese Revolution; Gandhi quarrels at Tolstoy farm with his son Harilal

1912 Gandhi tours South Africa with Gokhale; Wilson elected US president

1913 Protests Cape Supreme Court decree making Islamic marriages invalid; leads the "great march" satyagraha of over 2000 Indian coal miners and sugar plantation workers; Gandhi imprisoned

1914 Gandhi and General Jan Christiaan Smuts begin negotiations and reach compromise; Gandhi leaves South Africa for last time; returns to India via London; World War I begins

1915 Gandhi founds Ahmedabad ashrams, first Satyagraha ashram, then Sabarmati

1916 Wilson re-elected; Gandhi tours India and Burma

1917 Russian Revolution; US enters War; Gandhi takes up cause of indigo workers in Champaran, Bihar

1918 World War I ends; Gandhi leads satyagraha campaign for Ahmedabad textile workers

1919 Rowlatt Bills introduced to suppress seditious acts; nationwide hartal; Amritsar Massacre; Gandhi assumes editorship of the weekly Gujarati journal *Navajivan* and the English journal *Young India*

1920 Amritsar Congress; founds University of Gujarat; Harding elected US president

1921 Gandhi presides over bonfire of foreign cloth in Bombay; opens National College in Calcutta; Lord Reading becomes Viceroy of India; famine in USSR

1922 Chauri Chaura massacre of 21 Indian policemen; Gandhi suspends satyagraha; he is arrested and during the Great Trial sentenced to six years imprisonment; Mussolini to power in Italy

1924 Coolidge elected US President; Gandhi operated on for appendicitis; later released from prison; *Satyagraha in South Africa* serialized this year and the next in *Navijan* and *Young India*

1925 Gandhi creates All-India Spinning Association; his *Autobiography* begins to be serialized in *Navijan* and *Young India*; Madeleine Slade (Mirabehn) joins Gandhi's ashram; Scopes trial in Tennessee on teaching evolution

1927 Lord Irwin becomes Viceroy of India; Gandhi's A*utobiography* Vol. I is published; Lindbergh flies Atlantic

1928 Gandhi and colleagues achieve a victory helping Bardoli tenant farmers protest land taxes; his *Satyagraha in South Africa* is published; Hoover elected US president; Stalin rules USSR

1929 US stock market crash; depression begins; Gandhi's *Autobiography* Vol. II is published

1930 Declaration of the Independence of India; Gandhi leads Salt March from Sabarmati to Dandi; arrested and imprisoned at Yeravda without trial

1931 Gandhi released from jail; he negotiates with viceroy the Gandhi-Irwin Pact; attends the Round Table Conference in London; visits Romain Rolland in Switzerland; has a brief interview with Mussolini in Italy and visits the Vatican

1932–33 Protests against a separate electorate for the untouchables; imprisoned several times; fasts several times in protest to policies; advocates for untouchables; Roosevelt elected US President; Gandhi imprisoned in Yeravda Jail, 1932–33, and while in prison is allowed to begin editing the journal *Harijan* (the English-language edition), *Harijanbandhu* ("Brother to Harijans," the Gujarati edition), and *Harijan Sevak* ("Servant of Harijans," the Hindi edition)

1934 Leads new All-India Village Industries Association

1935 Gandhi's health declines

1936 Gandhi visited at Wardha by Margaret Sanger; oldest son Harilal becomes a Muslim; George V dies; Edward VIII becomes king but soon abdicates, and his younger brother George VI is crowned king

1939 Writes to Hitler, but letter remains undelivered; Neville Chamberlain replaced as British Prime Minister by Winston Churchill

1940 Begins campaign of individual civil disobedience against British war policy

1941 Writes a second letter to Hitler, which is also not delivered

1942 Launches "Quit India" campaign; leads nation-wide satyagraha campaign under the slogan "Do or Die"; arrested and imprisoned at Aga Khan Palace in Poona with Kasturba; Mahadev Desai, also in prison with them, dies of heart failure

1943 Fasts for twenty-one days as an appeal to the government for justice

1944 Kasturba dies at Aga Khan Palace; Gandhi released; begins talks with Jinnah to resolve Hindu-Muslim tensions

1945 Attends Simla Conference; Roosevelt dies and Truman becomes President; Churchill loses election for Prime Minister to Clement Attlee

1946 Visits Noakhali and other parts of Bengal to soothe Hindu-Muslim tensions

1947 Lord Mountbatten, last Viceroy, arrives in India; nation divided into India and Pakistan; Gandhi goes to Calcutta and promises to fast unto death to end violence

1948 Gandhi in New Delhi fasts for communal unity; bomb explosion at Birla House; ten days later, on January 30, Gandhi assassinated at Birla House

1.

Salt March and London Round Table 1930–1931

After Gandhi's release from Yeravda Prison in 1924, he needed time to reflect on the independence movement's setbacks and how he could best prepare the nation for the next steps. He found time to write his Autobiography: The Story of My Experiments with Truth *and* Satyagraha in South Africa. *But soon events created an opportunity for action.*

By 1927, the spirit of the national movement had begun to weaken, because of factions pulling in different directions and increasing tensions between Hindus and Muslims. But late in the year the British Government felt that a fresh review of the political situation was needed, and appointed the Simon Commission, with seven members, all British, to tour India and make constitutional proposals. The new Viceroy, Lord Irwin,[7] *perceiving himself as sympathetic to the oppressed and as more of a mediator than an autocrat, tried to bring together the various Indian leaders to prepare for the Commission's arrival in India in February 1928. But the Commission was boycotted by Congress and large groups of Muslims because all were offended by the Simon Commission's make-up, which implied that no Indians were capable of contributing to its proposals. There were violent demonstrations in Lucknow in August 1928, which were followed by an All-Parties Conference. The Conference approved a report drawn up by a committee headed by Motilal Nehru, which called for Dominion status (much like that of Canada at that time). Struggles continued, however, and another Congress in Lahore, in December 1929, called not for Dominion status, but for Independence, and authorized the launching of civil disobedience. On December 31, 1929, Jawaharlal Nehru hoisted the Tri-Color flag, signifying Indian independence. Gandhi proclaimed that people all over the country should fly the flag on January 26, 1930, and on that day take a pledge of independence, which he drafted and which "called British rule a 'four-fold disaster'—economic, political, cultural and spiritual" (Rajmohan Gandhi 302). The Congress Working Committee authorized Gandhi to begin civil disobedience when he thought the time was appropriate.*

7. Lord Irwin (Edward Frederick Lindley Wood, 1881–1959) had been a respected Conservative in the British Parliament and had served as president of the Board of Education and minister of Agriculture. He went on to serve as foreign secretary in the late 1930s under Neville Chamberlain and as ambassador to the United States during World War II (*Encyclopedia of India*).

Gandhi proposed to British Prime Minister Ramsay MacDonald[8] *an eleven point program, which listed what could be accomplished immediately in their demand for freedom. Everyone expected him to propose civil disobedience as the means of changing policy, but no one knew which demand he would choose as a focus. It was not* practical *to use civil disobedience on all eleven points; Gandhi decided to focus on a single issue, the fourth of the eleven demands—the abolition of the salt tax. Once this decision was shared with others, some of his own colleagues as well as British government leaders could not see how a protest of the salt tax could have much effect.*

The world he lived in was changing rapidly and drastically. The depression, which began with the New York stock market crash in October 1929, spread rapidly around the world, affecting people nearly everywhere, and altering economic and political policies. At the same time the rise of dictators in Europe presaged a world-wide war. The seven years between India's Declaration of Independence and the preliminary rumblings of World War II were Gandhi's most active and probably most effective time.

The Salt March (1930)

The Salt March deserves special treatment because of its importance as a mass political action and its significance in the Indian Freedom struggle. Gandhi had great hopes for the march to be more than a demonstration against one unfair tax; rather the march, he hoped, would initiate a nonviolent uprising that would bring the government to a standstill. Part of Gandhi's genius was his ability to create symbolic actions that could be easily communicated to millions of people. Such was the Salt March. It received attention across the nation and in the international media. It was understood by the illiterate masses and inspired them to action.

8. Ramsay MacDonald (1866–1937) became Britain's first Labor Party Prime Minister in the Labor governments of 1924 and 1929–1931; he served as Prime Minister of a coalition National Government 1931–1935 (www.britannica.com).

Salt was a necessity in India's climate. It could be, and often had been, made by simply raking up the salt on salt flats and beaches. Back in 1891, nearly forty years earlier, Gandhi in his first published article in The Indian Vegetarian *had written "There are thousands in India who have to live on one pice*[9] *a day. These live on bread and salt, a heavily taxed article." The tax on salt was only about three percent of the total tax revenue collected by the British, but it fell most heavily on those who were desperately poor. Lord Reading,*[10] *the previous Viceroy (1921–26), had had six interviews with Gandhi and tried hard to persuade Gandhi to accept British efforts at reform, but after the massacre at Jallianwala Bagh in Amritsar and the brutal repression by the British that followed, Gandhi now deeply mistrusted British efforts. Lord Reading went on to create a Tariff Board which abolished cotton excise taxes, allowed Indian mill owners to compete fairly with British textile manufacturers, but to reclaim lost revenue, Reading was also responsible for doubling the salt tax (*Encyclopedia of India*).*

Gandhi prefaced the campaign by writing a very long letter to Lord Irwin, then Viceroy (1926–31). The letter, from which excerpts are given below, was delivered in person by Reginald Reynolds, a young British Quaker who was residing at Gandhi's Sabarmati Ashram. Reynolds went on his errand dressed in khadi.[11] *It's worth noting that Gandhi saw Reynolds as more than a mere errand boy. Narayan Desai reports in his biography of his father, Gandhi's secretary Mahadev Desai,* The Fire and the Rose, *that Gandhi gave Reynolds much leeway in carrying out his mission, asking him to read the letter and deliver it only if he agreed with it. Desai adds that the Viceroy's Secretary sent a very rude reply, after which Gandhi said, "I asked for bread and received a stone instead" (448). In the letter Gandhi makes reference to a Round Table Conference, the first of the conferences that British Prime Minister Ramsay MacDonald convened, but then adjourned because of its failure to ensure Indian representation.*

---

9. pice: a very small coin (the modern rupee is divided into 100 pice)

10. Lord Reading (Rufus Isaacs, 1860–1935), a distinguished jurist, was Britain's Lord Chief Justice in David Lloyd George's cabinet, and the only person who was Jewish to serve as Viceroy of India (*Encyclopedia of India*).

11. khadi: handspun and hand-woven cloth, made famous by Gandhi

Letter to Lord Irwin

Satyagraha Ashram, Sabarmati
March 2, 1930

Dear Friend,

Before embarking on civil disobedience and taking the risk I have dreaded to take all these years, I would fain approach you and find a way out.

My personal faith is absolutely clear. I cannot intentionally hurt anything that lives, much less fellow human beings, even though they may do the greatest wrong to me and mine. Whilst, therefore, I hold the British rule to be a curse, I do not intend harm to a single Englishman or to any legitimate interest he may have in India.

I must not be misunderstood. Though I hold the British rule in India to be a curse, I do not, therefore, consider Englishmen in general to be worse than any other people on earth. I have the privilege of claiming many Englishmen as dearest friends. Indeed much that I have learned of the evil of British rule is due to the writings of frank and courageous Englishmen who have not hesitated to tell the unpalatable truth about that rule.

And why do I regard British rule as a curse?

It has impoverished the dumb millions[12] by a system of progressive exploitation and by a ruinous expensive military and civil administration which the country can never afford. It has reduced us politically to serfdom. It has sapped the foundation of our culture. And by the policy of cruel disarmament, it has degraded us spiritually. Lacking the inward strength, we have been reduced, by all but universal disarmament, to a state bordering on cowardly helplessness.

In common with many of my countrymen, I had hugged the hope that the proposed Round Table Conference might furnish a solution. But, when you said plainly you could not give any assurance that you or the British Cabinet would pledge yourselves to support a scheme of full Dominion Status, the Round Table Conference could not possibly forsake the solution for which

12. Gandhi uses the phrase "the dumb millions" to represent the toiling voiceless masses. In his day, "dumb" simply meant silent, speechless, voiceless, with no connotation of lack of intelligence.

vocal India is consciously, and the dumb millions are unconsciously, thirsting. Needless to say there never was any question of Parliament's verdict being anticipated. …

It seems as clear as daylight that responsible British statesmen do not contemplate any alteration in British policy that might adversely affect Britain's commerce with India or require an impartial and close scrutiny of Britain's transactions with India.

… Unless those who work in the name of the nation understand and keep before all concerned the motive that lies behind the craving for independence, there is every danger of independence coming to us so changed as to be of no value to those toiling voiceless millions for whom it is sought and for whom it is worth taking. It is for that reason that I have been recently telling the public what independence should really mean. …

The terrific pressure of land revenue, which furnishes a large part of the total, must undergo considerable modification in an independent India. Even the much vaunted permanent settlement benefits the few rich zamindars,[13] not the ryots.[14] The ryot has remained as helpless as ever. He is a mere tenant at will. … But the British system seems to be designed to crush the very life out of him. Even the salt he must use to live is so taxed as to make the burden fall heaviest on him, if only because of the heartless impartiality of its incidence. The tax shows itself still more burdensome on the poor man when it is remembered that salt is the one thing he must eat more than the rich man both individually and collectively. …

The matter resolves itself into one of matching forces. Conviction or no conviction, Great Britain would defend her Indian commerce and interests by all the forces at her command. India must consequently evolve force enough to free herself from that embrace of death.

It is common cause that, however disorganized and, for the time being, insignificant it may be, the party of violence is gaining ground and making itself felt. Its end is the same as mine. But I am convinced that it cannot bring the desired relief to the dumb millions. And the conviction is growing deeper and deeper in me that nothing but unadulterated non-violence can check the organized violence of the British Government. …

---

13. zamindars: landlords

14. ryots: peasants or tenant farmers

This non-violence will be expressed through civil disobedience, for the moment confined to the inmates of the Satyagraha Ashram, but ultimately designed to cover all those who choose to join the movement with its obvious limitations. …

… But if you cannot see your way to deal with these evils and my letter makes no appeal to your heart, on the 11th day of this month, I shall proceed with such co-workers of the Ashram as I can take, to disregard the provisions of the salt laws. … It is, I know, open to you to frustrate my design by arresting me. I hope that there will be tens of thousands ready, in a disciplined manner, to take up the work after me, and, in the act of disobeying the Salt Act to lay themselves open to the penalties of a law that should never have disfigured the Statute-book. …

This letter is not in any way intended as a threat but is a simple and sacred duty peremptory on a civil resister. Therefore I am having it specially delivered by a young English friend who believes in the Indian cause and is a full believer in non-violence and whom Providence seems to have sent to me, as it were, for the very purpose.

I remain,
Your sincere friend,
M. K. Gandhi

Gandhi launched the Salt March by speaking to those gathered at the ashram the night before they were to set off. The speech is an extraordinary statement of commitment and faith for Gandhi and his followers. It is important to note that Gandhi, in this political action, sees himself as a religious leader. He knew that the act of collecting salt in defiance of British law would have far-reaching consequences, and he vowed not to return to Sabarmati until India had won independence. In preparation, his core of ashram marchers were given strict rules for how to handle violence and arrest, and each took a solemn vow. Although Gandhi says that 72 men were joining the march, he was joined initially by some 78 followers, and those following him soon numbered in the thousands. Robert Payne notes that the procession was nearly two miles long (390).

Speech at Prayer Meeting

Sabarmati Ashram

[March 12, 1930]

God willing, we shall set out exactly at 6.30. Those joining the march should all be on the spot at 6.20. If our first step is pure, all our subsequent steps will be good and pure. As Manilal is joining us, I would say something for his benefit. He should not join just because he is my son though he cannot help being my son, nor can I forget that I am his father.

We who are setting out with a great responsibility on our heads—we the Ashram inmates—have but one capital. We can boast of no learning. We who took certain vows and pledged ourselves to the Ashram way of life ought to adhere to those vows scrupulously. The seventy-two men joining the march should once again read the Ashram rules and think whether or not they should join the march. Those inmates of the Ashram who have dependents will not be able to draw money from the Ashram for them. None should join the struggle with that hope. This fight is no public show; it is the final struggle—a life-and-death struggle. If there are disturbances we may even have to die at the hands of our own people. Even in that case, we shall have made our full contribution to the satyagraha struggle. We have constituted ourselves the custodians of Hindu-Muslim unity. We hope to become the representatives of the poorest of the poor, the lowest of the low and the weakest of the weak. If we do not have the strength for this, we should not join the struggle. For my part I have taken no pledge not to return here, but I do ask you to return here only as dead men or as winners of swaraj.[15] Chhaganlal Joshi[16] will not be able to run up here if Dhiru falls ill. Even if the Ashram is on fire, we will not return. Only those may join, who have no special duty to their relatives. The marchers have vowed to follow life-long

15. swaraj: "self-rule"; used by Indian nationalists to denote independence from Britain; used by Gandhi to mean political and economic independence, as well as self-discipline

16. Chhaganlal Joshi: the manager of Sabarmati ashram, who would walk just behind Gandhi (Rajmohan Gandhi 308)

poverty and to observe brahmacharya[17] for life. They leave here with the determination to observe brahmacharya and will remain faithful to that determination. The man who always follows truth and always proclaims what he does is a brave man. Anyone who deceives others is not brave. I cannot speak to anyone privately for I have not a minute to spare. Though addressing myself to Manilal particularly, I say this to all.

We are entering upon a life-and-death struggle, a holy war; we are performing an all-embracing sacrifice in which we wish to offer ourselves as oblation. If you prove incapable, the shame will be mine, not yours. You too have in you the strength that God has given me. The Self in us all is one and the same. In me it has awakened; in others, it has awakened partially.

A huge procession joined the marchers in departing Sabarmati at 6:30 AM, remaining together until they reached Chandola lake at 8:30 AM. He and his followers knew better than anyone the drama and high stakes involved; "For me there is not turning back," Gandhi said. On March 29 at Bhatgam he said, "I would rather die a dog's death and have my bones licked by dogs than that I should return to the ashram a broken man!" (Payne 391). Here at Chandola on the first day of the March, Gandhi directed a parting message to those who would be returning to Sabarmati.

Parting Message at Chandola

March 12, 1930

Your surpassing love for me has drawn you thus far. I appreciate your affection for me which has been so vividly demonstrated by you. … There were rumours of my arrest last night. God is great, mysterious indeed are His ways. I am here to say good-bye to you. But even if I were in prison, with your strength I could come back. Indeed, it is your strength that will bring us swaraj. Go back and resolve to do your share. Propagate khaddar[18] work, be

17. brahmacharya: celibacy; chastity in quest for God; used by Gandhi to mean control not only of the sexual appetite but control of all the senses, hence freedom from desire and lust

18. khaddar: another word for khadi (homespun cotton cloth)

prepared to offer yourselves as civil resisters. Let there be no flinching. Your way at present, however, lies homeward; mine straight on to the sea-coast. You cannot accompany me at present, but you will have an opportunity to accompany me in a different sense later. …

During the Salt March, Gandhi delivered the following speech at Broach (summarized in Young India, *April 3, 1930, under the title "Hindu-Muslim Question"). In his introductory note in* Young India, *Gandhi expressed the importance of this speech dealing with "the communal question." The fuller version, below, was collated with the Gujarati version. (CWMG 48:477n1). When Gandhi mentioned "this white beard," he pointed towards Abbas Tyabji, a Muslim and an old friend. If he should die during the march, Gandhi had planned for Abbas Tyabji to lead the procession. Their friendship went back to 1896, when Tyabji, a respected judge, was among those who had supported Gandhi's efforts to publicize conditions in South Africa, and they had served together in 1919 on a committee studying conditions in the Punjab. When Gandhi was arrested on May 5, 1930, Tyabji, who was then 75, took over leadership of the marchers for their nonviolent raid on the Dharsana salt depot. Their relationship underscored Gandhi's lifelong experience and vision of Hindu-Muslim unity. In the following speech, he took this opportunity to respond to those wishing to undermine Hindu intentions toward Muslims. The problem of keeping unity or giving in to separation, Gandhi called "the question of questions" (Rajmohan Gandhi 78, 213, 266, 315).*

Speech at Broach

March 26, 1930

Chandubhai has asked for my blessings. But who am I to give blessings? … I hope that by the time I reach Dandi the blessings I am receiving at every village on this march will have added up to such a mountain that even this monster of a Government will cower at the sight.

A Muslim youth has sent me questions on the Hindu-Muslim problem. One of them is: "Do you expect to win swaraj through your own single effort or assisted merely by the Hindus?"

I have never dreamt that I could win swaraj merely through my own effort or assisted only by the Hindus. I stand in need of the assistance of Mussalmans,[19] Parsis, Christians, Sikhs, Jews and all other Indians. I need the assistance even of Englishmen. But I know too that all this combined assistance is worthless if I have not one other assistance, that is, from God. All is vain without His help. And if He is with this struggle, no other help is necessary.

But to realize His help and guidance in this struggle, I need your blessings, the blessings of all communities. The blessings of thousands of men and women belonging to all communities that have attended this march are to me a visible sign of the hand of God in this struggle.

I know that there are occasions when the hand of God has to be traced in the curses of men. But this is not such an occasion. Today I am doing what the nation has been yearning for during the past ten years. Have I not been rebuked for delaying civil resistance? Have not friends angrily said, "You are stopping the progress of the nation towards its goal? You have only to say, 'Let there be civil resistance,' behold! there is swaraj." There is some truth in the taunt. Full civil resistance does mean swaraj. But I was staying my hand. I had no confidence in myself. I was straining my ear to listen to the still small voice within, but only up to yesterday there was no response. It was in Lahore I had told a journalist that I saw nothing on the horizon to warrant civil resistance. But suddenly, as in a flash, I saw the light in the Ashram. Self-confidence returned. Englishmen and some Indian critics have been warning me against the hazard. But the voice within is clear. I must put forth all my effort or retire altogether and for all time from public life. I feel that now is the time or it will be never.

And so I am out for battle and am seeking help on bended knee from this white beard as also the little girls. For in this battle even they can help; and thank God, they are eager to do so. I have insistent letters from them demanding enlistment.

Thus the answer to the Muslim youth's question is complete. I need the help of all races and from all climes.

---

19. Mussalman: archaic for a follower of Islam, a Muslim

A satyagrahi[20] has no power he can call his own. All the power he may seem to possess is from and of God. He therefore moves toward his goal carrying the world's opinion with him. Without the help of God he is lame, blind, groping.

Ever since 1921 I have been reiterating two words, "self-purification" and "self-sacrifice." God will not assist him without these two. The world is touched by sacrifice. It does not then discriminate about the merits of a cause. Not so God. He is all-seeing. He insists on the purity of the cause and on adequate sacrifice therefor.

The question was put by a Mussalman representing a powerful interest. But had a little Parsi girl representing but a hundred thousand Parsis asked the question, I should have given the same answer and said: "Without the help of Parsis there is no swaraj." I am thankful to be able to say that I have had during the march abundant proof of the blessings of these communities. I have read friendliness in the eyes and in the speech of the Mussalmans who along with the rest have lined our route or attended the meetings. They have even given material aid.

Yet I know that I have not the Ali Brothers with me.[21] Maulana Shaukat Ali will no longer have me in his pocket. Do not think, I do not miss him. I hold no distinction between him and [a] blood brother. His resistance therefore can only be short-lived. If truth is in me, the Brothers must capitulate. They cannot long keep out of the battle. I crave too the assistance of Englishmen. It was neither empty formula nor a touch of vanity that prompted me to send an English friend with my letter to the Viceroy. But choosing Reginald Reynolds as my messenger, I sealed the bond between them and me. For my enmity is not against them, it is against their rule. I seem to be born to be an instrument to compass the end of that rule. But if a hair of an English head was touched I should feel the same grief as I should over such a mishap to my brother. I say to them as a friend: "Why will you not understand that your rule is ruining this country? It has got to be destroyed even though you may pound us to powder or drown us. We must declare what we feel...."

---

20. satyagrahi: someone who practices satyagraha

21. The Ali brothers were two Muslim leaders who cooperated with Gandhi on a number of issues.

Civil resistance will merely give the power to the nation to assert her will. But when the time comes for its assertion, the document embodying the will will have to be sealed by all the communities. Thus without the co-operation of all the communities, there is no Independence.

But what should we do meanwhile? We must at least be true to the salt we eat. Her starving millions are the salt of India's earth. To be true to them we must free the salt from a tax which they have to pay equally with the rich and in the same proportion as the rich. In our ignorance we have been paying this inhuman imposition. Having realized our folly we will be traitors to the starving millions if we submit to the exaction any longer. …

This is the English translation of a message dictated by Gandhi at Dandi, the place where the march ended on the sea coast. At this point the marchers, steadily increasing in numbers, had been walking for over a month.

Message to the Nation

Dandi
April 9, 1930

At last the long expected hour seems to have come.

In the dead of night my colleagues and companions have roused me from deep slumber and requested me to give them a message. I am, therefore, dictating this message, although I have not the slightest inclination to give any.

Messages I have given enough already. Of what avail would this message be if none of the previous messages evoked a proper response? But information received until this midnight leads me to the belief that my message did not fall flat, but was taken up by the people in right earnest. The people of Gujarat seem to have risen in a body as it were. I have seen with my own eyes thousands of men and women at Aat and Bhimrad fearlessly breaking the Salt Act. Not a sign of mischief, not a sign of violence have I seen, despite the presence of people in such large numbers. They have remained perfectly peaceful and non-violent, although Government officers have transgressed all bounds.

Here in Gujarat well-tried and popular public servants have been arrested one after another, and yet the people have been perfectly non-violent. They have refused to give way to panic, and have celebrated the arrests by offering civil disobedience in ever increasing numbers. This is just as it should be.

If the struggle so auspiciously begun is continued in the same spirit of non-violence to the end, not only shall we see Purna Swaraj[22] established in our country before long, but we shall have given to the world an object-lesson worthy of India and her glorious past. . . .

On May 5, the authorities finally arrested Gandhi under Regulation 25, a law dating back to 1827 that was thought to be no longer in use, allowing the government to arrest anyone thought to be an undesirable element or a threat. There would be no trial. The following account appeared in The Bombay Chronicle.

Arrest at Midnight

Karadi

May 5, 1930

The Magistrate proceeded to Gandhiji's[23] hut and woke him up. "I have a warrant for your arrest, Mr. Gandhi," said the Magistrate.

Gandhiji asked politely:

I am not surprised, but will you read out the warrant to me?

The Magistrate complied with this request and read the following which was signed by Sir Frederick Sykes, Governor of Bombay.

"Whereas the Government view with alarm the activities of Mr. M.K. Gandhi, they direct that he should be placed under restraint under Regulation 25 of 1827 and suffer imprisonment during the pleasure of the Government and be immediately removed to the Yeravda Central Jail."

Gandhiji was smiling when the warrant was being read. He said:

"I am prepared to accompany you, but will you allow me to have a wash and clean my teeth?" "With pleasure," said the Magistrate.

22. Purna Swaraj: complete independence

23. Gandhiji: "ji" is added after names as an expression of reverence and respect.

In the meantime, the whole Ashram was up, and everyone was anxious to have a parting 'darshan'[24] of Gandhiji. Having finished his wash, Gandhiji came out of the cottage to say his prayers. The whole Ashram knelt down to recite the prayers while the police officers watched. Gandhiji himself led the chorus. He then collected his papers and gave them in charge of a volunteer whom he had chosen as Captain during his incarceration.

Upon arriving at Yeravda after a journey by train and car, Gandhi gave the following interview to a reporter from The Daily Telegraph. *He expresses his simplicity as well as his ability to be centered, even as he was about to be imprisoned.*

Interview to *The Daily Telegraph*

Borivli
May 5, 1930

Gandhi seemed surprised when he saw my companion and myself, for both of us were known to him. He greeted us in the most friendly manner.

"Have you a farewell message you would like to give, Mr. Gandhi?" I asked. He replied:

Shall I give it now or shall I wait?

"You had better give it now," I replied.

He paused, seeming to be at a loss for words and somewhat dazed by events. Then he answered:

Tell the people of America to study the issues closely and to judge them on their merits.

"Have you any bitterness or ill will towards anyone?" I asked.

None whatsoever; I had long expected to be arrested.

"Do you think your arrest will lead to great disturbances throughout India?"

No, I do not; in any case I can honestly say that I have taken every possible precaution to avert disturbances.

Then you anticipate no troubles?

24. darshan: blessing obtained by being in the presence of someone or something revered

The Mahatma[25] hesitated for a moment and then replied:

I hope not; I have done my best to prevent them.

At this point the law intervened. Inspector Gordon stepped forward, saying, "Now, Mr. Gandhi, if you are ready, please." Only one person accompanied Gandhi from the train, a doctor of the Indian Medical Service, who remained silent in the background. He now took his seat alongside the prophet, with Inspector Gordon sitting by the chauffeur.

In the following letter Gandhi is making arrangements for his stay in prison at Yeravda. Gandhi is an experienced prisoner, who is being treated carefully, but who wants to make some points with his jailers. Later E.E. Doyle, who would be promoted to colonel and Inspector General of Prisons, hand delivered the Yeravda Agreement, also known as the Yeravda Pact, to Gandhi in 1932 during his fast to end untouchability.

Letter to E. E. Doyle

Yeravda
May 10, 1930

Dear Major Doyle,

Having thought over our conversation, I have come to the conclusion that I must avoid, as much as possible, the special privileges offered to me by the Government.

Books and newspapers I do not want through the Government. Of newspapers, I would send for these if permitted:

The Bombay Chronicle,
The Times of India,
Indian Social Reformer,
Modern Review,
Young India and *Navajivan* (Hindi and Gujarati)

If these are allowed, I take it that they will not be mutilated.

25. Mahatma: great soul; after returning to India in 1915, Gandhi was honored with the title of "Mahatma" by various people including Rabindranath Tagore, Gandhi's friend and 1913 winner of the Nobel Prize for literature. (Rajmohan Gandhi 180; Payne 290).

The Government have suggested Rs[26] 100 as monthly allowance. I hope I shall need nothing near it. I know that my food is a costly affair. It grieves me, but it has become a physical necessity with me.

Neither you nor the Government will, I hope, consider me ungrateful for not accepting all the facilities offered to me. It is an obsession (if it is to be so called) with me that we are all living at the expense of the toiling semi-starved millions. I know too that the saving caused by my economy can but be an infinitesimal drop in the limitless ocean of waste I see going on around me, whether in prison or outside of it—much more out of it. I admit nevertheless it is given to man only to do very little. He dare not omit to do that little.

Again, I hold radical views about prison treatment.

I have never taken kindly to the classification recently made. I hold that a murderer is just as much entitled to have his needs supplied as any other prisoner. What is therefore needed is not a mechanical makeshift, but a human adjustment. . . .

A year after the Salt March, Gandhi wrote the following brief letter to those who went to Dandi. The letter, most of which is quoted below, reveals much about Gandhi's relationship with his fellow marchers.

For the Dandi Pilgrims

May 14, 1931

All the fellow pilgrims who undertook the march to Dandi on 12th March 1930 being scattered all over and not being in constant touch with me, it is necessary to remind them through these columns that they are still under the same discipline and vows that they took before beginning the march and after. They are therefore expected to keep an accurate diary of the day's work from day to day, to attend to the two prayers, to keep their wants as low as possible and therefore to keep their diet as simple as possible and to do the daily sacrificial spinning. Those who are living in villages can conduct village schools, teaching the children in addition to a knowledge of the three R's,

26. Rs: rupees (the common currency of India)

hand-spinning and other processes of cotton, insisting on their attendance to personal hygiene and village games and athletics, doing village cleaning themselves, seeking at the same time the assistance of the villagers and their children and collecting and tabulating all the necessary information about the villagers. The workers would also find out those using foreign cloth and intoxicating drinks and drugs and try to wean them from both by paying them friendly visits and otherwise creating public opinion in the villages in these matters. They will wherever possible and necessary organize peaceful picketing. Of course they would seek to remove untouchability. The workers should send to Sjt. Chhaganlal Joshi a report every month of their work including an abstract from their diary. Needless to say they are expected to keep an accurate account of every pice they may spend and receive. …

The London Round Table Conference (1931)

By June 30, 1930, the government had jailed all of the Congress leaders, but the Congress continued to operate. The government arranged for the leading members of Congress to meet in jail, but they avoided helping the government out of the mess it found itself in. By early 1931, Lord Irwin had decided that something must be done. In mid-February 1931, he brought Gandhi to the Viceroy's House to see if they could find some kind of truce. Over the next days, Gandhi and Lord Irwin worked out a compromise agreement known as the Gandhi-Irwin Pact. One result was that Gandhi was authorized to attend the second Round Table conference, to be held in London. The first, which was held in India, had been boycotted by the Congress party. Gandhi attended sessions faithfully and spoke often. He had very little hope that the proceedings would be significant. He was determined, however, to renew contacts in Britain, and to talk with British mill owners and workers who saw his activities in India as a cause of unemployment in Britain.

The excerpts are from letters, interviews, and other documents and, separately, entries from the diary Gandhi kept. For Gandhi, this was not only a political journey—which turned out to be a failure—but also a return to the city where he had lived for nearly three years as a law student, visited several times during his South African years on political business, and had spent several months on his way back to India from South Africa.

Gandhi arrived in London in the afternoon, and as noted in the Collected Works, *"though it was raining, the rush of people was so great that police precautions became necessary. He was driven straight to Friends House at Euston Road"* (CWMG-CD *53:348n1). Laurence Housman, the British playwright and Quaker who drove him from Folkestone to Friends House, welcomed him on behalf of the reception Committee saying "You are a strange man, Mr. Gandhi! You are so sincere, you embarrass us; so simple, you baffle us" (Muzumdar and Durant 136; Hunt 180). Gandhi used this opportunity to state Congress's instructions as well as to express ideas on his mind.*

Speech at Friends House

London
September 12, 1931

You will not this evening expect me to take up much of your time, or to say much with reference to my mission, but I wish to say one thing in a general way. I am here with my friends on a mission of peace. I am, and my friends are, guests of the great English nation. I hope that by the time we have finished our work, you will not consider that we have in any way abused your hospitality. I hope that, as the days go by, you will understand the scope of the mission on which the Congress has sent me. You will also please know that, as an agent holding a power of attorney from the Congress, I shall have my limitations. I have to conduct myself within the four corners of the mandate that I have received from the Congress. There are some words in that mandate which give me a little measure of freedom of action, but in all respects, in all fundamental respects, I am hidebound. I may not, if I am to be loyal to the trust reposed in me, walk outside the four corners of that mandate.

I venture to feel that Congress stands for a good cause, of which any nation would be proud. The Congress wants freedom unadulterated for the dumb and starving millions. In order that Congress may represent them, the Congress has chosen, as its means of vindicating this freedom, truth and non-violence.

I am fully aware that not all Congressmen have lived up to the means, and I know that we of the Congress shall deserve the curses of the whole world if, in the name of truth and non-violence, we do the contrary. But I derive the greatest consolation from the knowledge that I possess that the best workers of the Congress today represent truth and non-violence in their essence. . . .

We have in our midst, I know, a school of violence also. I know many of these young men—I have lived with them, I have mixed with them, I have talked to them also. I have endeavoured, as several others of their co-workers have endeavoured, to win them from what we hold is an error; but, at the same time, I know that there is a common cause, even between them and ourselves. They are burning to attain the freedom to which India is entitled, which is India's birthright. I repeat what I have told them in public and in private—that their activities embarrass Congress, their activities set back the hands of the clock of progress. The Congressmen who are wedded to this creed realize fully that these young men, who resort to violence for the sake of gaining freedom, do harm not only to themselves but to the country, and most of all to the dumb millions to whom I have referred.

We may be nationalists, we may be ardent patriots, but immediately we apply these means of truth and non-violence, our patriotism becomes internationalism. Our patriotism is so conceived that we want our freedom not to injure the freedom of any other country or of any single individual. We believe not in the law that might is right, or the greatest good of the greatest number, but we believe in the greatest good of all, including the meanest of creatures amongst all God's creation. And if India could vindicate her freedom, attain it through these means, do you not think that it would be well, not only with India, but with the whole world? . . .

This is a reporter's account of an interview, printed in The Sunday Times *and* The Tribune, *given the same day as the speech at Friends House. It is interesting to compare them.*

Interview to the Press

London

September 12, 1931

Mr. Gandhi, in an interview, gave me the essence of the Congress mandate which he will present. It lays down:

1. The Congress goal is complete independence.

2. This means control over the army, external affairs, finance and economic policy.

3. Scrutiny by an impartial tribunal of the financial transactions of the British Government.

There were words, he said, which gave him a small measure of freedom of action, but otherwise he was bound to the four corners of the mandate.

Mr. Gandhi also said that, baffling though it was, he would never despair of arriving at some workable solution of the Hindu-Muslim question. …

He was always optimistic. He was prepared to go the "whole hog" with the Muslims without the slightest reservation. He would sign a blank paper and leave the Muslims to write in what they considered the truth, and he would then fight for it.

Mr. Gandhi stipulated that any demands by Mohammedans must be on behalf of the whole of them, adding:

"I say this purposely because there is a small body—how large I do not know—which is called the Nationalist Muslim Party. I cannot be false to that party."

His business was to bring the two parties of Muslims together.

In the following broadcast which was made from Kingsley Hall on the Columbia Broadcasting Service, Gandhi summarizes his views on what is happening and should happen for the world—or at least the American part of it—as he appeals for the support of "the conscience of the world." The "Indian Conference" in the first sentence refers to The Roundtable Conference. Apparently unaccustomed to speaking on the radio, he said before beginning, "Do I have to speak into that?" and when he finished with the address, listeners heard him also say, "Well that's over" (CWMG-CD *53:353n1). Despite this awkwardness, the address covers a number of important issues.*

Broadcast to America

September 13, 1931

In my opinion, the Indian Conference bears in its consequences not only upon India but upon the whole world. India is by itself almost a continent. It contains one-fifth of the human race. It represents one of the most ancient civilizations. It has traditions handed down from tens of thousands of years, some of which, to the astonishment of the world, remain intact. No doubt the ravages of time have affected the purity of that civilization, as they have of many other cultures and many institutions.

If India is to perpetuate the glory of her ancient past, it can do so only when it attains freedom. The reason for the struggle having drawn the attention of the world, I know, does not lie in the fact that we Indians are fighting for our liberty, but in the fact that the means adopted by us for attaining that liberty are unique and, as far as history shows us, have not been adopted by any other people of whom we have any record.

The means adopted are not violence, not bloodshed, not diplomacy as one understands it nowadays, but they are purely and simply truth and non-violence. No wonder that the attention of the world is directed towards this attempt to lead a successful, bloodless revolution. Hitherto, nations have fought in the manner of the brute. They have wreaked vengeance upon those whom they have considered to be their enemies.

We find in searching national anthems adopted by great nations that they contain imprecations upon the so-called enemy. They have vowed destruction and have not hesitated to take the name of God and seek Divine assistance for the destruction of the enemy. We in India have reversed the process. We feel that the law that governs brute creation is not the law that should guide the human race. That law is inconsistent with human dignity.

I, personally, would wait, if need be, for ages rather than seek to attain the freedom of my country through bloody means. I feel in the innermost recesses of my heart, after a political experience extending over an unbroken period of close upon thirty-five years, that the world is sick unto death of blood-spilling. The world is seeking a way out, and I flatter myself with the belief that perhaps it will be the privilege of the ancient land of India to show that way out to the hungering world.

I have, therefore, no hesitation whatsoever in inviting all the great nations of the earth to give their hearty co-operation to India in her mighty struggle. It must be a sight worth contemplating and treasuring that millions of people have given themselves to suffering without retaliation in order that they might vindicate the dignity and honour of the nation.

I have called that suffering a process of self-purification. It is my certain conviction that no man loses his freedom except through his own weakness. I am painfully conscious of our own weaknesses. We represent in India all the principal religions of the earth, and it is a matter of deep humiliation to confess that we are a house divided against itself; that we Hindus and Mussalmans are flying at one another. It is a matter of still deeper humiliation to me that we Hindus regard several millions of our own kith and kin too degraded even for our touch. I refer to the so-called "untouchables."

These are no small weaknesses in a nation struggling to be free. You will find that, in this struggle through self-purification, we have assigned a foremost [part of our] creed to the removal of this curse of untouchability and the attainment of unity amongst all the different classes and communities of India representing the different creeds. ...

There is a force which has a constructive effect and which has been put forth by the nation during this struggle. That is the great care for the semi-starved millions scattered throughout the 700,000 villages dotted over a surface 1,900 miles long and 1,500 miles broad. It is a painful phenomenon that these simple villagers, through no fault of their own, have nearly six months of the year idle upon their hands.

The time was not very long ago when every village was self-sufficient in regard to the two primary human wants: food and clothing. Unfortunately for us, the East India Company,[27] by means I would prefer not to describe, destroyed that supplementary village industry, and the millions of spinners who had become famous through the cunning of their deft fingers for

27. East India Company: Established in 1600 by Royal Charter, the East India Company extended trade to India, and became increasingly powerful by working with Mughal emperors and Indian merchants. The British Parliament changed the structure of the company in 1784, giving the British government control over its possessions in India. In 1858, the British Crown replaced the East India Company with the Government of India (*Historical Dictionary of India*).

drawing the finest thread, such as has never yet been drawn by any modern machinery. The village spinners found themselves one fine morning with their noble occupation gone. From that day forward India has become progressively poor.

No matter what may be said to the contrary, it is a historical fact that, before the advent of the East India Company, these villagers were not idle, and he who wants may see today that these villagers are idle. It, therefore, required no great effort or learning to know that these villagers must starve if they cannot work for six months in the year.

May I not, then, on behalf of these semi-starved millions, appeal to the conscience of the world to come to the rescue of a people dying for regaining its liberty?

In his opening speech to the Round Table Conference, Gandhi emphasizes the ties among all parties at the conference, Hindus, Muslims, Parsis, and Christians, and the benefits of their finding a way for a unified India to remain a partner with Great Britain. He acknowledges the important connection between Great Britain and India, and states that "I prided myself on being… a British subject," yet now "I would far rather be called a rebel than a subject." Not unlike Thomas Jefferson in the US Declaration of Independence, Gandhi says, that when one people violate their relationship with another people, "Either party should have the right to sever the connection." Covering the Round Table Conference and following Gandhi's other recent speeches, William Shirer observed that Gandhi spoke from the heart and that this speech was "the greatest one of his long political life" (Shirer 141; Rajmohan Gandhi 330-31).

Opening Speech to the Round Table Conference

London

September 15, 1931

Time was when I prided myself on being, and being called, a British subject. I have ceased for many years to call myself a British subject; I would far rather be called a rebel than a subject. But I have aspired—I still aspire—to be a citizen, not of the Empire, but in a Commonwealth; in a partnership if possible—if God wills it, an indissoluble partnership but not a partnership superimposed upon one nation by another. … [E]ither party should have the right to sever the connection, to dissolve the partnership. …

I wondered, even as I was sailing towards London, whether we in the Committee at the present moment would not be a drag upon the British Ministers—whether we would not be interlopers. And yet I said to myself: It is possible that we might not be interlopers. …

India, yes, can be held by the sword! I do not for one moment doubt the ability of Britain to hold India under subjection through the sword. But what will conduce to the prosperity of Great Britain, the economic freedom of Great Britain—an enslaved but rebellious India, or an India an esteemed partner with Britain to share her sorrows … ?

And so I said to myself whilst I was nearing the shores of your beautiful island, per chance it might be possible for me to convince the British Ministers that India as a valuable partner, not held by force but by the silken cord of love—an India of that character might conceivably be of real assistance to you in balancing your Budget, not for one occasion but for many years. What cannot two nations do—one a handful, but brave, with a record for bravery perhaps unequalled, a nation noted for having fought slavery, a nation that has at least claimed times without number to protect the weak—and another a very ancient nation, counted in millions, with a glorious and ancient past, representing at the present moment two great cultures, the Islamic and Hindu cultures. … And supposing that God fires both Hindus and Musslmans represented here with a proper spirit, so that they close ranks and come to an honourable understanding—take that nation and this nation together, and I again ask myself and ask you whether, with an India free, completely independent as Great Britain is, whether an honourable partnership between these two cannot be mutually beneficial, even in terms of the domestic affairs of this great nation.

The Conference of Missionary Societies was held at Church Missionary House in London. There was no detailed report to the press, but Gandhi gave an interesting account of how he felt about missionary endeavors in India. In the excerpts that follow, he criticizes missionary work, yet acknowledges some benefits, and refers to Charlie Andrews[28] as a model of Christian understanding.

Speech at Conference of Missionary Societies

London

October 8, 1931

... The idea of converting people to one's faith by speech and writings, by appeal to reason and emotion and by suggesting that the faith of his forefathers is a bad faith, in my opinion, limits the possibilities of serving humanity. I believe that the great religions of the world are all more or less true and that they have descended to us from God. Having come to us, however, through human media, they have become adulterated. Holding this belief, I hold also that no religion is absolutely perfect. In the bosom of God there is nothing imperfect, but immediately it comes through a human medium, it constantly suffers change and deterioration. The seeker after truth most humbly recognizes this possibility. I have found that the progress of truth is impeded by the spoken word which is the limitation of thought, for no man has been able to give the fullest expression in words to thought. The very nature of thought is limitless and boundless.

A man of prayer believes that God works in a mysterious way and wants the whole world to possess the truth he himself has seen. He would simply pray for it to be shared. It passes; it takes wing.

Shall I use a simile of which I am never tired and which you will forgive. Religion is like a rose. It throws out the scent which attracts us like a magnet and we are drawn to it involuntarily. The scent of religious contact has a greater pungency than the scent of the rose, that is why I hold my view with reference to conversion. It is good and proper that, when we feel satisfied that we have found God and that God has spoken to us, we should wish to

---

28. Charles (Charlie) Freer Andrews (1871–1940), an Anglican missionary and priest, was deeply influenced by Rabindranath Tagore and the progressive nationalist G. K. Gokhale, who also advised and was much admired by Gandhi. Charlie Andrews worked closely with Gandhi in South Africa during 1914–15, again during the Round Table Conference, and after (*Oxford Dictionary of National Biography*).

share that mystery, but as God has spoken to us mysteriously, we should allow that God Mystery to flow from us in exactly the same manner.

Whilst I criticize this part of missionary work, I willingly admit that missions have done indirect good to India. There is no doubt about this. But for my having come under Christian influence, some of my social work would not have been done. My fierce hatred of child marriage—I gladly say—is due to Christian influence. I have come into contact with many splendid specimens of Christian missionaries. In spite of differences I could not possibly help being affected by their merit. …

Before I knew anything about Christianity I was an enemy of untouchability. I could not understand my mother, whom I adored, withdrawing the hem of her garment from the untouchables. My feelings gained momentum owing to the fierce attack from Christian sources on this evil.

If I want a pattern of the ideal missionary, I should instance C.F. Andrews. If he were here, he would blush for what I want to say. I believe that he is today truer, broader and better for his toleration of the other principal religions of the world. He never speaks with me about conversion to Christianity though we are the closest friends. … If you asked me whether I have noticed any laxity or indifference about his own fundamental position, I would say that he has become firmer in his own faith and in the growth of love for others. I think, whereas he used to see blemishes in Hinduism, today perhaps he sees those very blemishes in another setting, and therefore becomes more approachable to the Hindu. He is today a potent instrument in influencing the lives of Hindus for the better in hundreds and thousands of cases.

His Indian friends in South Africa wrote to me that he was Deenbandhu—brother of those in distress. He has endeared himself even to the scavenger class, the pariahs. He went to them naturally and influenced their conduct in the simplest manner, and now he is held in very great affection. …

I want to put all my cards on the table and I want you to do so too. I hope you will be able to say, "We listened to the old man that evening and we heard nothing that was not truthful and sincere."

A meeting was held at Woodbrooke, a Quaker center near Birmingham. Horace Alexander, who had worked with Gandhi in India and become his close friend, chaired the meeting. Those in attendance included the Mayor of Birmingham, the Lady Mayoress, and the Bishop of Birmingham. Gandhi's speech and his replies to questions are forthright, and often amusing. He speaks as one who feels he is among people who will understand him, though the questions are not always wholly friendly. All British Friends were not in favor of Gandhi's goals and methods, but Gandhi seems at home in his replies. To answer the last question he outlines the history of satyagraha, and explains non-violence and the power of suffering.

Speech at Birmingham Meeting

Selly Oak, Birmingham

October 18, 1931

Whereas to other places I have gone as a matter of business, to deliver my message, I have come here as a matter of pilgrimage because this Settlement it was that spared and sent Mr. Horace Alexander to us at a time when we were in need of a friend. … It was a time when news of satyagraha could not be transmitted from India, everything that was sent was censored, the principal men were all in jail. It was then that the Friends came to the conclusion that a mission ought to be sent to India and Mr. Alexander was chosen for that purpose. Not only were you able to spare him but his wife, a cripple, spared him. Now you will understand why it is a pilgrimage for me to come here.

With regard to the work before me, I did not think I should take your time to describe it to you now. The vast majority of the people now know what the Indian National Congress claims for the nation. You know what means we have adopted, perhaps, for the first time in history, to achieve our independence. And you also know how far the nation during the last year was able to live up to its creed. I would like to emphasize upon you the fact that, if the work that is now being done at the Round Table Conference is to bear fruit, it will do so only if the pressure of intelligent public opinion is brought to bear upon it. I have often remarked that my true work in England lies outside the Conference, not in the Conference. In my few public speeches I have not hesitated to throw out a hint that no work was being done in the Conference, that it was marking time and that the precious time of those who had come from India and those who were representing British interests in the Conference was being wasted. That being my opinion, I cannot be too insistent that responsible leaders of public opinion in the British Isles should inform themselves of the true nature of the struggle that Indians are carrying on against heavy odds. For, unless you understand the true nature and the inner meaning of this struggle, you will not be able to bring effective pressure to bear on those who are conducting the affairs of State here.

I know enough of the composition of this meeting to know that you are all earnest seekers after truth and anxious to do the right, not only especially in regard to this, but any cause that deserves the assistance of human beings. And if you will approach this question from this standpoint, it is just likely that the deliberations of the Round Table Conference might prove fruitful. . . .

The speech was followed by a number of questions from the audience. Three of Gandhi's answers are included here.

One member of the audience asked the question whether the Round Table Conference had broken down and whether India should wait for swaraj until another conference.

[Gandhi replied:]

I am not giving up all hope till I have severed all connection with the Round Table Conference. Apparently, therefore, I still entertain some hope though, I may say, I have little data to build on. But it is against my nature to violently break away from an organization with which I have been co-operating. I do not know whether, the next time when the solution comes, there will be another Round Table Conference or not, but this much I know, that if the Round Table Conference breaks down, a solution will not be reached before India has passed through a fiery ordeal much more severe than the one it passed through last year. . . .

An amusing question was asked by a friend who quoted a letter from *The Manchester Guardian* in which the correspondent questioned Gandhiji's authority to speak for the untouchables, as he belonged to the priestly class which had kept that community depressed so far, and asked whether Gandhiji himself was not a great hindrance in the way of a settlement.

[Gandhi replied:]

I never knew that I was a Brahmin,[29] but I do happen to be a Bania,[30] which is certainly regarded as a term of painful reproach. But let me inform the audience that my community excommunicated me when I came to English shores 40 years ago and the work that I have been doing entitles me to be called a farmer, weaver and untouchable. I was wedded to the work for the extinction of untouchability long before I was wedded to my wife. There are two occasions in our joint life when there was a choice between working for the untouchables and remaining with my wife and I would have preferred the first. But thanks to my good wife, the crisis was averted. In my Ashram, which is my family, I have several untouchables and a sweet but naughty girl living as my own daughter. As to whether I am acting as a hindrance to a settlement, I confess, I am for the simple reason that I would not be satisfied with any compromise short of real complete independence for India.

[A questioner asked:]

... What is it that makes you sometimes feel that appeal to reason should be put aside in favour of more drastic action?

[Gandhi replied:]

Up to the year 1906 I simply relied on appeal to reason. I was a very industrious reformer.... But I found that reason failed to produce an impression when the critical moment arrived in South Africa. My people were excited—even a worm will and does sometimes turn—and there was talk of wreaking vengeance. I had then to choose between allying myself to violence or finding out some other method of meeting the crisis and stopping the rot, and it came to me that we should refuse to obey legislation that was degrading and let them put us in jail if they liked. Thus came into being the moral equivalent of war. I was then a loyalist, because I implicitly believed that the sum total of the activities of the British Empire was good for India and for 'humanity.' Arriving in England soon after the outbreak of the War,

29. Brahmin: member of the highest caste sanctioned by Hinduism; literally one who knows Brahman, the Supreme Being.

30. Bania: member of a subgroup of the third caste, the Vaishyas, comprised of businessmen, merchants, herders, and farmers. The four main castes, or varnas, are Brahmin, Kshatriya, Vaishya, and Shudra. Below the four varnas are untouchables, also known as Harijans or Dalits.

I plunged into it and later, when I was forced to go to India as a result of the pleurisy that I had developed, I led a recruiting campaign at the risk of my life, and to the horror of some of my friends.... And so, in 1920, I became a rebel. Since then the conviction has been growing upon me, that things of fundamental importance to the people are not secured by reason alone, but have to be purchased with their suffering. Suffering is the law of human beings; war is the law of the jungle. But suffering is infinitely more powerful than the law of the jungle for converting the opponent and opening his ears, which are otherwise shut, to the voice of reason. Nobody has probably drawn up more petitions or espoused more forlorn causes than I, and I have come to this fundamental conclusion that, if you want something really important to be done, you must not merely satisfy the reason, you must move the heart also. The appeal of reason is more to the head, but the penetration of the heart comes from suffering. It opens up the inner understanding of man. Suffering is the badge of the human race, not the sword.

This interview with the Associated Press focuses on Gandhi's economic views and on technology. The interviewer, Harold Callender (1892–1959), was the much respected European correspondent of the New York Times. *Callender had earlier met Ford in America and heard him put forward the view that demand for cheaper things would stimulate mass production (*CWMG-CD *54:21n2). Gandhi had been thinking about issues of economic growth, state-controlled industry, village labor, and international trade as early as 1909 when he wrote* Hind Swaraj. *As a result of this interview, Callender wrote an article entitled "Gandhi Dissects the Ford Idea," which appeared in the* New York Times Magazine, *November 8, 1931.*

AP Interview with Callender

London
October 16, 1931

Q. Do you feel, Gandhiji, that mass production will raise the standard of living of the people?

A. I do not believe in it at all. There is a tremendous fallacy behind Mr. Ford's reasoning. Without simultaneous distribution on an equally mass scale, the production can result only in a great world tragedy. Take Mr. Ford's cars. The saturation point is bound to be reached soon or late. Beyond that point the production of cars cannot be pushed. What will happen then?

Mass production takes no note of the real requirement of the consumer. If mass production were in itself a virtue, it should be capable of indefinite multiplication. But it can be definitely shown that mass production carries within it its own limitations. If all countries adopted the system of mass production, there would not be a big enough market for their products. Mass production must then come to a stop. …

The interviewer then asked Gandhi whether Russia was not a country that had developed mass production without exploiting … the less industrialized nations, or without falling into the pit of unequal distribution.

A. In other words, you want me to express opinion on State-controlled industry, i.e., an economic order in which both production and distribution are controlled and regulated by the State as is being done today in Soviet Russia. Well, it is a new experiment. How far it will ultimately succeed, I do not know. If it were not based on force, I would dote on it. But today, since it is based on force, I do not know how far and where it will take us.

Q. Then, you do not envisage mass production as an ideal future of India?

A. Oh yes, mass production, certainly, but not based on force. After all, the message of the spinning-wheel is that. It is mass production, but mass production in people's own homes. If you multiply individual production to millions of times, would it not give you mass production on a tremendous scale? But I quite understand that your 'mass production' is a technical term for production by the fewest possible number through the aid of highly complicated machinery. I have said to myself that that is wrong. My machinery must be of the most elementary type which I can put in the homes of the millions. Under my system, again, it is labour which is the current coin, not metal. Any person who can use his labour has that coin, has wealth. He converts his labour into cloth, he converts his labour into grain. If he wants paraffin oil, which he cannot himself produce, he uses his surplus grain for getting the oil. It is exchange of labour on free, fair and equal terms—hence it is no robbery. You may object that this is a reversion to the primitive system of barter. But is not all international trade based on the barter system? …

The Round Table Conference had failed. Gandhi's farewell address to the conference is remarkably blunt. He states where he stands with regard to coming decisions, explains the importance of Congress's representation, and states the power of civil disobedience to which "governments have to succumb." Rajmohan Gandhi writes that this speech "must be unique in the story of empires" given Gandhi's forthright assessment of Great Britain's failure, and, in essence, his announcement of his next assault. Samuel Hoare, the Secretary of State for India, said of Gandhi's farewell speech, "With an eye and mind as pointed as a needle, he penetrated in a moment any sham" (Rajmohan Gandhi 336-37).

Farewell Speech to the Round Table Conference

London
December 1, 1931

I live under no illusion. I do not think that anything that I can say this evening can possibly influence the decision of the Cabinet. ...

All the other parties at this meeting represent sectional interests. Congress alone claims to represent the whole of India, all interests. ... Congress knows no distinction of race, colour or creed; its platform is universal. It may not always have lived up to the creed. I do not know a single human organization that lives up to its creed. ... But the worst critic will have to recognize, as it has been recognized, that the National Congress of India is a daily-growing organization, that its message penetrates the remotest village of India. ...

Congress ... has been accused of running or desiring to run a parallel Government; and in a way I have endorsed the charge. If you could understand the working of the Congress, you would welcome an organization which could run a parallel Government and show that it is possible for an organization, voluntary, without any force at its command, to run the machinery of Government even under adverse circumstances. ...

I heard several speakers ... saying what a dire calamity it would be if India was fired with the spirit of lawlessness, rebellion, terrorism and so on. I do not pretend to have read history, but as a schoolboy I had to pass a paper in history also, and I read that the page of history is soiled red with the blood of those who have fought for freedom. I do not know an instance in which nations have attained to their own without having to go through an incredible measure of travail. The dagger of the assassin, the poison bowl, the bullet of the rifleman, the spear and all these weapons and methods of destruction have been up to now used by what I consider blind lovers of liberty and freedom, and the historian has not condemned him. …

The Congress then comes upon the scene and devises a new method not known to history, namely, that of civil disobedience. … But again I am up against a stone wall and I am told that that is a method that no Government in the world will tolerate. … No government may tolerate civil disobedience, but governments have to succumb even to these forces. …

A nation of 350 million people does not need the dagger of the assassin, it does not need the poison bowl, it does not need the sword, the spear or the bullet. It needs simply a will of its own, an ability to say "No", and that nation is today learning to say "No". …

This is, perhaps, the last time that I shall be sitting with you at negotiations … my thanks to all—from Their Majesties down to the poorest men in the East End, where I have taken up my habitation.

In that settlement which represents the poor people of the East End of London I have become one of them. They have accepted me. …

… from high to low I have found nothing but the utmost courtesy and the utmost affection. I consider that it was well worth my paying this visit to England in order to find this human affection. It has enhanced, it has deepened my irrepressible faith in human nature that although Englishmen and Englishwomen have been fed upon lies so often that I see disfiguring your Press, that although in Lancashire the Lancashire people had perhaps some reason for becoming irritated against me, I found no irritation, no resentment even in the operatives. The operatives, men and women, hugged me. … I shall never forget that.

I am carrying with me thousands upon thousands of English friendships. I do not know them, but I read that affection in their eyes as early in the morning I walk through your streets. All this hospitality, all this kindness will never be effaced from my memory no matter what befalls my unhappy land. I thank you for your forbearance.

Gandhi kept a diary in 1931 which begins after he had been in England for over a month. There are daily entries from October 14 to December 31.

Entries below show what Gandhi's life was like during these hectic weeks and the items he felt worth noting: his travels, his visits to schools and universities, the range of people with whom he met, his spiritual practice, his state of health, and state of mind. More footnotes are included below than for other selections to identify many of the references and names. One can see from Gandhi's meetings outside of the Round Table Conference how he was not only in dialogue with government officials such as Prime Minister Ramsay McDonald, but also how he was making the most of his time to develop third-party support. Later entries record his return journey by way of the continent where he spent some time with Romain Rolland, the novelist and pacifist who had written a book-length biography of Gandhi published in 1924. They had corresponded; Rolland had encouraged Madeleine Slade, the British admiral's daughter, to join Gandhi. At age thirty-three, she joined the ashram in 1925 and Gandhi gave her the name Mirabehn. This was Rolland and Gandhi's first and only meeting. He also went to Rome, where he met Mussolini but not the Pope, though he did visit the Vatican. He was not as impressed by Michelangelo's frescoes as he was by a tall crucifix in the Sistine Chapel. His trip back through the Suez Canal may remind readers of his youthful journey to England in 1889 which he had described in the Autobiography. *As he approached Bombay, he became more and more aware of how complete the failure of the Conference had been. He began hearing that many of his friends and supporters had been jailed, and that he would also be imprisoned shortly after his arrival.*

London, October 14, Wednesday

Spun 180 rounds. Discussion about the army with persons called together by Sir Samuel Hoare; talk with Benthall; talk with Jinnah.[31]

London, October 15, Thursday

Spun 176 rounds. Talk with Sir Samuel Hoare; talk with Sapru, Jayakar[32] and others, also students' function. Talk with Latifi.

London, October 16, Friday

Spun 162 rounds. The Conference, Press lunch, Mussalmans, India Office, Prohibition meeting, Nawab Saheb. Now it is 1 o'clock.

Birmingham, October 17, Saturday

Spun 127 rounds. Speech for gramophone recording; Madgaonkar; reprimanded Maud for renting a house; visit to Nottingham, Birmingham in the evening. Andrews arrived; Devdas returned to Knightsbridge.[33]

---

31. According to Babubhai Patel, a veteran khadi worker, one round is equal to one meter of hand spun thread, and 4000 of hand spun thread is one meter of cloth. By recording how much he had spun that day, Gandhi expressed the importance he placed on spinning as a daily practice (Usha Thakkar, Mani Bhavan Gandhi Sangrahalaya, correspondence with editors). Sir Samuel Hoare (1880–1959) was the British Secretary of State for India and later the British Foreign Secretary and British Home Secretary (www.nndb.com); Muhammad Ali Jinnah (1876–1948), the leader of India's Muslim League, advocated for Pakistan as a separate nation for Muslims, contrary to Gandhi's vision of a united India; upon the nation's creation in 1947, Jinnah became Pakistan's first Governor General (www.storyofpakistan.com). At the time of the Round Table Conference, Jinnah was residing in London (Hunt 207).

32. Tej Bahandur Sapru was the lawyer and Liberal leader who in 1928 "urged Congress to concede to Jinnah's demands and 'be finished with it;'" Sapru's colleague M R Jayakar was a barrister from Bombay who had served in 1919 with Gandhi on a committee investigating the Hunter Commission's terms of inquiry into the Amritsar Massacre. Sapru and Jayakar played an important role in arranging negotiations for the Gandhi-Irwin Pact of 1931. (Rajmohan Gandhi 213, 297, 321).

33. Devadas (Devdas) Gandhi (1900–1957) was Gandhi's fourth and youngest son.

Birmingham, October 18, Sunday

Spun 129 rounds. Bishop Barnes; the Steiner School; Dr. Parghi, meeting of members of Ashram.[34]

London, October 20, Tuesday

Spun 176 rounds. Upton Close called; Archbishop of Canterbury, Samuel Hoare, Elmhurst; meeting at Chatham House.[35]

Eton, October 23, Friday

Spun 221 rounds. Spoke on Federal Structure Committee [the Round Table Committee on which Gandhi served] on Federal Court; visited Agricultural Exhibition in the evening. Then had a talk with Sapru and others. Went to Eton [the elite preparatory school] at night. Spoke to youths there.

Oxford, October 24, Saturday

Spun 162 rounds. Left Eton in the morning; arrived at Oxford. On the way called at the house of Col. Maddock. Then lunched at the house of Mira's uncle. Spent two hours with the Fellows at Oxford. Later at night in the Indian Majlis. Lala Dunichand's son called.[36]

---

34. Ernest Barnes (1874–1953), Bishop of Birmingham, was a controversial and outspoken pacifist; Rudolf Steiner (1861–1925) inspired a world-wide movement of Steiner Schools founded upon his progressive theories of universal human values and educational pluralism giving "equal attention to the physical, emotional, intellectual, cultural and spiritual needs of each pupil" (www.steinerwaldorf.org). Gandhi felt strongly about education and had attempted to educate his sons himself. This meeting with Steiner as well as the meeting with Maria Montessori (see below, October 28) were very likely of special interest to all three. "Ashram" presumably refers to the Friends center at Woodbrooke (see above "Speech at Birmingham Meeting," October 18, 1931).

35. Upton Close was a British writer and admirer of Gandhi (Rajmohan Gandhi 611); Chatham House, founded in 1920, was established to promote free speech and confidentiality at meetings dealing with international affairs (www.chatham house.org).

36. Majlis: an assembly; in this case, "a mainly Muslim association of Indians in Britain" (Rajmohan Gandhi 335). Lala Dunichand, of Lahore, was the Punjab Congress President (Deep Chand Bandhu, *History of Indian National Congress* 114).

Oxford, October 25, Sunday

Spun 199 rounds. In the morning at Thompsons' met Prof. Murray, Sadler and others.[37] Then met Sir Henry Lawrence, Mrs. Elwin, the Ruskin Society, then discussion with Oxford dons; at night with the Rhodes scholars.[38]

London October 28, Wednesday

Spun 181 rounds. Met Madame M..., Madame Montessori,[39] Mira's illness.

London, October 29, Thursday

Spun 215 rounds. Could not rise today at 3 o'clock. Was late by an hour. Many persons called. Felt mentally agitated. Talked with Dutta. Met Sapru

37. Gandhi spent two weekends at Oxford and one at Cambridge. At one gathering, including Gilbert Murray, Sir Michael Sadler, and others, the host Edward Thompson observed that Gandhi was questioned for three hours: "It was a reasonably exacting ordeal, yet not for one moment was he rattled or at a loss, The conviction came to me, that not since Socrates has the world seen his equal for absolute self-control and composure" (Hunt 196-97). Gilbert Murray, in the *Hibbert Journal* in 1918, had predicted that Gandhi would be "a dangerous and uncomfortable enemy" to the government "because his body, which you can always conquer, gives you so little purchase upon his soul" (qtd. in Erikson 391).

38. The Ruskin Society was founded by scholars and devotees of John Ruskin, whose *Unto This Last*, in its teaching on the value and equality of all people's labor, had significant influence on Gandhi (*Autobiography: Or My Experiments with Truth* 264-65).

39. Maria Montessori, MD (1870–1952) was the first woman in Italy to receive a medical degree. During World War II, Montessori was forced to leave fascist Italy and went to India to continue her work. She wrote that "... education is not what the teacher gives; education is a natural process spontaneously carried out by the human individual, and is acquired not by listening to words but by experiences upon the environment. The task of the teacher becomes that of preparing a series of motives of cultural activity, spread over a specially prepared environment, and then refraining from obtrusive interference" (www.montessori.edu/maria.html). Mahadev Desai recorded that Montessori wrote a note about their meeting, which said, "Gandhi appears to me as a soul rather than a body," and Desai added that "Gandhiji explained... that Madame Montessori respects the child's personality, and respecting a person, is non-violence" (Narayan Desai 518).

and others at Malaviyaji's, met Strakosch and Sir Basil Blackett in the evening. At night met Baba and other youths.[40]

London, October 30, Friday

Spun 182 rounds. Vegetarian lunch, meeting with Layton. The Commonwealth of India League.

Cambridge, October 31, Saturday

Spun 162 rounds. Met Quaker friends. Met Sardar Ujjal Singh at Cambridge at 5 o'clock.[41]

Cambridge, November 1, Sunday

Spun 192 rounds. Visited Pemberton College in the morning. Present at the meeting held there were Lowes Dickinson, Evelyn Wrench and others. The discussion lasted three hours. Then made a few visits. Saw Andrews's old room, visited King's Chapel. In the evening Nicholson called. At night meeting of the Indian Majlis. Commenced silence at 9:38 p.m.[42]

London, November 4, Wednesday

Spun 173 rounds. The Conference; Sir Daniel Hamilton;[43] to Malavijayi's, doctor's, Turkish general.

---

40. As early as 1915, Gandhi had worked with Pandit Madan Mohan Malaviya (1861–1946), a Brahmin who supported the Indian National Congress (Rajmohan Gandhi 184). Sir Basil Blackett (1882–1935) served during the 1920s as Finance Member to the Government of India (JSTOR).

41. Sardar Ujjal Singh (1895–1983), a Sikh representative to the Round Table Conference, was elected to the Punjab Legislative Council in 1926 and became a member of the Viceroy's Consultative Committee on Reforms (www.sikhiwiki.org).

42. Goldsworthy Lowes Dickinson (1873–1932) was an historian from Cambridge University and lectured at the London School of Economics (http://janus.lib.cam.ac.uk); Evelyn Wrench (1882–1966) founded the English Speaking Union in 1918 to foster Anglo-American friendship, in 1930 founded the All People's Association to promote friendly relations among peoples, and was editor of the *Spectator* magazine 1925–32 (www.esu.org).

43. Sir Daniel Hamilton (1860–1939) was a Scottish businessman and partner in Mackinnon, Mackenzie & Co., Calcutta, a shipping and trading company; he worked to improve living conditions of the poor in India (*Who's Who 1937*).

London, November 5, Thursday

Spun 220 rounds. The Emperor's party; met the members of the Postal Workers' Union; Sidney Walton.

London, November 6, Friday

Spun 172 rounds. Bernard Shaw and his wife called. Sir Darcy Lindsay called. Meeting with Sir John Maynard, Sapru and others; Letter to Mac Donald; Jaiji came with me at night.[44]

Oxford, November 7, Saturday

Spun 208 rounds. Reached Oxford at 11 o'clock in the morning. Had talk with Malcolm MacDonald, Prof. Murray. Andrews arrived in the evening; at night had talk with Lord Lothian,[45] Coupland was present.

---

44. George Bernard Shaw (1856–1950), who had won the Nobel Prize in Literature in 1925, shared with Gandhi long-time interests in socialist ideas and vegetarianism. "Sir John Maynard" presumably refers to John Maynard Keynes (1883–1946), the economist whose theories where hugely influential during the 20th century. In *The Economic Consequences of the Peace*, published in 1919, Keynes foresaw that punitive reparations imposed on Germany by the Allies would create political instability. His later writings advocated government spending during economic downturns to counter unemployment and, at a time in history when balanced budgets were the norm, he advocated deficit spending (www.econlib.org). Jaiji Jehangir Petit was Chair of the Bombay Women's Committee for Women's Suffrage (Geraldine Forbes, Women in Modern India 95).

45. Lord Lothian (Philip Kerr, 1882–1940), a world federalist, would write *Pacifism Is Not Enough* (1935) and became the British Ambassador to the US 1939–1940 (www.oxfordreference.com).

London, November 9, Monday

Spun 192 rounds. Came to London from Oxford. Wrote a number of letters. Purushottamdas's party; talk with Corbett; prayer and dinner at Rameshwardas's, meeting at Friends' House, Reynolds called on me.[46]

London, November 10, Tuesday

Spun 203 rounds. Sapru and others came. Talked with them. Met Corbett and Mrs. Subbaroyan. London School of Economics, Holborn Restaurant.[47]

---

46. The meeting at Friends House, November 9, was organized by the Fellowship of Reconciliation (*CWMG-CD* 54:335n1). According to James Hunt, Horace Alexander had proposed weekly prayer meetings at Friends House beginning September 30, 1931, in order to promote communication and understanding among Hindus, Muslims, as well as Quakers. Gandhi attended several of these meetings, the last being on December 2. Hunt writes, "As the decade of the thirties wore on... Quakers in England and America found in satyagraha a deeper dimension to their own peace witness, and experimented with its application in a wide range of situations, both domestic and international. The Meeting of the Friends and Gandhi in 1931 was an important moment in that process of the cross fertilization of eastern and western thought" (204).

47. In the *Autobiography*, Gandhi describes how in 1888 at the Holborn Restaurant, which he then called "palacial," his friend Shukla had rebuked his manners; Gandhi happily left without eating and waited outside the restaurant for his friend; the Holborn Restaurant in 1891 was the site of his farewell speech to the Vegetarian Society—a speech at which Gandhi felt he had failed (*Autobiography* 44, 54; Hunt 222).

London, November 13, Friday

Spun 147 rounds. The Minority Committee, Smuts, the Aga Khan[48] and others. Mr. Benn and others, Smuts, Lansbury, the Westminster School, Birla, representative of the News Chronicle.[49] Now it is midnight.

London, November 17, Tuesday

Spun 178 rounds. The Committee, the Prime Minister, Smuts, Cornett, Lothian, Lady Astor, Benthall and others.

London, November 18, Wednesday

Spun 167 rounds. Rev. Hayes, Philip, the Committee, Women's meeting, Lloyd George for three and a half hours. Now it is 1 o'clock.[50]

London, November 19, Thursday

Spun 183 rounds. The Committee, Brockway, speech in the Committee on racial discrimination and communal differences.

---

48. Jan Christiaan Smuts (1870–1950) was Colonial Secretary in Louis Botha's South African government in 1908 when he and Gandhi were adversaries over Indian rights in South Africa. In 1916 Smuts became a lieutenant-general in the British Army and served in Lloyd George's War Cabinet during World War I. He returned to South Africa in 1919, becoming Prime Minister. Although Gandhi and Smuts opposed each other, in 1913, while in the South African Bloemfontein Jail, Gandhi made a pair of sandals for General Smuts as an expression of friendship. They stayed in contact over the next decades and Smuts returned the sandals to Gandhi in 1939 for his seventieth birthday (Oxford Reference Online; Payne 271-72). The Aga Khan III, Sultan Muhammad Shah (1885–1957) was the head of the world's Shia Ismaili Muslims, and led the Muslim delegation at the Round Table Conference (www.ismaili.net). The Aga Khan Palace in Pune was taken over by the British for their use during World War II, and was used in 1942 to imprison Gandhi, Kasturbai, and Mahadev Desai (Rajmohan Gandhi 471).

49. G.D. (Ghanshyam Das) Birla (1894–1983) was an industrialist who became one of Gandhi's close associates; Gandhi was staying at Birla's home in New Delhi in 1948 when he was assassinated (http://encycloindia.com).

50. David Lloyd George (1863–1945) was the British Prime Minister 1916–1922.

London, November 25, Wednesday

Spun 160 rounds. Made two speeches in the Committee. Mirza and Dr. Ambedkar[51] came in the evening. Visited a Catholic church.

London, November 27, Friday

Spun 174 rounds. Andrews left for South Africa. Met Samuel Hoare. Went to Bhandari's; then met Lansbury.

London, November 28, Saturday

Spun 174 rounds. The Plenary Session. Hoare consulted me about a resolution to thank His Majesty the King-Emperor. I declined to be present. Cables to Vallabhbhai and Satis Babu.[52]

London, November 30, Monday

Spun 157 rounds. Made a day-long speech in the Committee. Reached home at 3 o'clock in the morning. Meeting at Horrabin's at 8.30.[53]

---

51. Bhimrao Ramji Ambedkar (1891–1956), despite being an untouchable who was raised in poverty, overcame many obstacles, to study at the University of Bombay and Elphinstone College, and to study abroad at Columbia University and the London School of Economics. Upon returning to India he became the relentless champion for the untouchables and the disadvantaged. Disillusioned with Hinduism's entrenched caste system, Dr. Ambedkar advocated that the untouchables must determine their own independence. He fought for the protection of the Depressed Classes through the establishment of reserved seats in the government, which Gandhi objected to, and he objected to Gandhi's use of the term "Harijan." Despite their clashes and disagreements, Gandhi advocated for Dr. Ambedkar's place in independent India's government, where he served in the first cabinet and chaired the committee drafting the Constitution (*Concise Oxford Dictionary of Politics*; www.ambedkar.org; Rajmohan Gandhi 598-99).

52. Sardar Vallabhbhai Patel (1875–1950), Gandhi's close political ally, studied law in London, and was imprisoned in 1930 during the Salt March; he became known as "iron man of India" and was highly instrumental in the formation of the Indian government; at Gandhi's request, Sardar Patel stepped aside to allow Nehru to become the first Prime Minister (www.culturalindia.net).

53. J. F. Horrabin (1884–1962) was a Labour Member of Parliament, a journalist and cartoonist.

London, December 1, Tuesday

Spun 184 rounds. The Conference concluded. Had a talk with Sapru and others. Also with Carr and Benthall.

London, December 2, Wednesday

Spun 166 rounds. Felt feverish today. Attended the Quakers' silent worship.

Paris, December 5, Saturday

Spun 151 rounds. Left London in the morning. Am accompanied by Evans, Rogers, Maud, Muriel, Shamrao.[54] Reached Paris in the evening. A big crowd there. A reception by the Indians.

Villeneuve, December 6, Sunday

Spun 167 rounds. Left Paris in the morning. Muriel stayed behind. Arrived at Villeneuve in the evening. Meeting with Rolland, with journalists.

Villeneuve, December 7, Monday

Spun 185 rounds. From 10 to 12:30 with Rolland. Did not go for a walk in the morning because of the rain but had sound sleep. When the sun appeared in the afternoon, I went for a stroll. Wrote letters to Hoare in the evening. Cable from Vallabhbhai, replied to it. Cable to Sir Jagdish Bose, to Ghose.

---

54. Sergeants Evans and Rogers were assigned by Scotland Yard to protect Gandhi. "The two went wherever Gandhi went, and kept the long hours he did. … Gandhi usually worked past midnight and slept … about four hours a night." Upon his return to India and before his arrest one week later, Gandhi sent Evans and Rogers two watches, which he said to his aides had to be English (Rajmohan Gandhi 331, 340-41). "Muriel" presumably refers to Muriel Lester (1885–1968), the founder of the settlement house, Kingsley Hall, in the poor district of the East End where Gandhi stayed during the Round Table Conference. James Hunt describes Kingsley Hall as founded by committed pacifists, "a disciplined community of prayer, service, and voluntary poverty, it was a veritable Christian ashram" (181); Lester was instrumental, particularly in 1946–1947 when Gandhi persuaded Nehru and Patel to offer Dr. Ambedkar a place in India's first cabinet (Rajmohan Gandhi 598).

Villeneuve, December 8, Tuesday

Spun 170 rounds. Spent two and half hours in the morning with Rolland. Three meetings in the afternoon in Lausanne. Returned at midnight.

Villeneuve, December 9, Wednesday

Spun 160 rounds. Visited a poor woman's house and International Sanatorium; held prayers at Romain Rolland's house. Presented a shawl from Madame Cama to Madeleine Rolland.

Villeneuve, December 10, Thursday

Spun 204 rounds. Meeting in Geneva, talks with Rolland, speech at a Chillon School, talk with Toma, talk with the Arabs.

On Way to Rome, December 11, Friday

Spun 178 rounds. Talk with Rolland; Sir Cowasji met me. Left Villeneuve at 2.30. Girls from Indu's school called. Was provided a State car in Milan. Large crowds had gathered on the way.

Rome, December 12, Saturday

Spun 204 rounds. Arrived at Rome at 8.30 in the morning. Received letter to the effect that the Pope could not receive me. Three of us stayed with General Moris, the others in a hotel. Went to see the Vatican in the afternoon. At 6 o'clock Mussolini. £ 20 to Maud.

On Way to Brindisi, December 13, Sunday

Spun 180 rounds. Tolstoy's daughter came in the morning; schools for young people, concessions to women, the forum, a gathering at Scarpa's, the Princess called and Amanullah's secretary. Left at 10.40 at night. The Privats are with me.

On Board Ship, December 14, Monday

Spun 137 rounds. Reached Brindisi in the morning. Evans, Rogers returned. S.S. Pilsna sailed at 12.30. The deck is no good, hence there will be some inconvenience. It is quite cold here. Vithalbhai is with me.

On Board Ship, December 17, Thursday

Spun 190 rounds. Arrived at Port Said at 11 o'clock. Sindhis[55] and Egyptians came to fetch me. But as there was no halt at Suez, I could not go. The Sindhis presented me a purse of about Rs. 1,500.

On Board Ship, December 18, Friday

Spun 162 rounds. Left Suez at 5.30. Justice Holland, Lalkaka and others met me. Read the bhajans revised by Hoyland.[56]

On Board Ship, December 19, Saturday

Spun 170 rounds. Commenced writing with the right hand from today. Slept thrice during the day. Wrote letters. Read Hoyland's book, *The Cross Moves East.*

On Board Ship, December 21, Monday

Spun 170 rounds. We are nearing Aden. Was able to sleep a little less during the day today. Wrote an article for *Indian News.* Wrote letters. Completed the one to Mussolini.

On Board Ship, December 22, Tuesday

Spun 175 rounds. Arrived at Aden at 12.30 in the morning; went ashore; there was a meeting; visited Suraj's residence. Met the Resident Col. Riley. Returned to the ship at 4.30. Collected about Rs. 4,000. Today I have a pain in the left side of the chest. The steamer weighed anchor at 5 o'clock.

---

55. People from the Sindh region of Pakistan, located south of Punjab

56. bhajans: devotional songs. John S. Hoyland created an English rendering of hymns from the Ashram Bhajanvali; this was a collection of devotional songs, made by Gandhi during his detention in Yeravda prison during the previous year (*CWMG-CD* 54:339n1). While staying as Woodbrooke, Gandhi met Hoyland, and as the next diary entry mentions, while on shipboard, Gandhi read Hoyland's *The Cross Moves East: A Study in the Significance of Gandhi's Satyagraha* (Hunt 203).

On Board Ship, December 25, Friday
Spun 171 rounds, Am reading report of the House of Commons debate on the Prime Minister's speech at the Round Table Conference. Had a talk with Masani in the evening.[57]

Bombay, December 28, Monday
Spun 184 rounds. Arrived at Bombay in the morning. Great welcome, mammoth meeting, the Welfare League, etc.

Bombay, December 29, Tuesday
Spun 189 rounds. Talked with Subhasbabu,[58] representatives of Andhra, Karnatak, etc. The Working Committee, telegram to the Viceroy letter to Sir Fazli.

Bombay, December 30, Wednesday
Spun 214 rounds. The Stree Seva Dal in Matunga, talked with Raghvir Singh, the Working Committee, the doctor examined me. Visited Sir Chinubhai and enquired about his health. Talked with Jamnadas, with Kaka, with Jayaprakash.[59]

Bombay, December 31, Thursday
Spun 177 rounds. The Viceroy's telegram arrived. Sent a reply. Completed drafting of a resolution at 1.30 a.m. in the night. Then spun. Now it is 2.45.

---

57. This is likely Minoo Masani, who, while in prison in India in 1934, helped form a Socialist Party; this faction hoped to become a party within Congress but met opposition from Congress's leaders: Sardar Vallabhbhai Patel, Chakravarti Rajagopalachari (C R), Rajendra Prasad, and Jawaharlal Nehru (Rajmohan Gandhi 368).

58. Subhas Chandra Bose (1897–1945) was president of the Indian National Congress in 1938 and 1939, but resigned from the Congress because of his differences with Gandhi. The government imprisoned him in his own house in Calcutta, but he escaped, traveled to Germany and founded a nationalist force called the Indian National Army (www.gandhi-manibhavan.org).

59. Stree Seva Dal: a women's group doing grassroots social work. Jayaprakash (JP) Narayan (1902–79) became an earlier follower of Gandhi, left to study at several US universities, including the University of Wisconsin where he became interested in Marxism, and returned to India to become an important leader in the independence movement and later Indian politics (www.mkgandhi-sarvodaya.org).

Lalji Sheth, Modi called.[60] Recited morning prayers today on the way, then went to visit the Sevikas. Held the evening prayer in the Lady Northcote Orphanage.

The telegram to the Viceroy, which Gandhi mentions above, read as follows:

Gandhi/Viceroy Telegrams

December 31, 1931

"I was unprepared on landing yesterday to find Frontier and U.P. ordinances shootings in Frontier and arrests of valued comrades in both on top of the Bengal Ordinance awaiting me. I do not know whether I am to regard these as indication that friendly relations between us are closed or whether you expect me still to see you and receive guidance from you as to the course I am to pursue in advising the Congress. I would esteem a wire in reply."

The Viceroy's reply was not encouraging, and Gandhi wired back indicating his intention to carry out further civil disobedience.

60. Sheth and Modi likely refer to Lalji Naranji Sheth and H.P. Modi. Sheth was President of Indian Merchants' Chamber, Bombay, and Modi was President, Bombay Millowners' Association (Usha Thakkar, Mani Bhavan Gandhi Sangrahalaya, correspondence with editors).

2.

A New Journal, a New Cause, and a New Ashram

1932–1936

When Gandhi returned from Europe, he walked into a changed political climate. The Second Round Table Conference had failed, and British authorities had chosen to take a hard line. Many Indian leaders had already been jailed, and on January 4, 1932, seven days after his return, Gandhi was arrested, and detained in Yeravda Prison in Pune. He carried on his political activity as well as he could, but did not become seriously involved until September. Ramsay MacDonald, the British Prime Minister, announced a decision to establish a separate electorate for the "Depressed Classes," meaning the untouchables. Dr. Ambedkar, the leader of the untouchables, had advocated such an arrangement. The proposal moved Gandhi to take steps even in prison to prevent this outcome, which he saw as undermining a unified Hinduism and a unified India.

On September 20, 1932, he began a "fast unto death" not only to protest the proposed policy but also to awaken the conscience of Hindus regarding untouchables. British authorities and others were alarmed at the possibility that Gandhi would die in prison. By September 26th, he was in very serious condition. His weight had dropped from a normal 110 pounds to 95 pounds, and he was hovering between consciousness and unconsciousness. Dr. Ambedkar was extremely stubborn in negotiations, but British authorities proposed a compromise which included the statement that "henceforth, amongst Hindus no one shall be regarded as an untouchable." After a period of great tension, the Yeravda Pact, as it was called, was delivered to Gandhi, who lay on his cot in the Yeravda courtyard. The pact was signed by leaders of the untouchables and of caste Hindus. Gandhi was convinced by those with him that this was the best agreement they were likely to get, and he decided to break his fast. In his biography of Gandhi, Yogesh Chadha observes, "As usual, he would yield unexpectedly on details, so long as he saved the principle" (328). Because of his fast, all over India untouchables had been welcomed into Hindu temples. The change, however, was temporary. Gandhi had not succeeded in ending untouchability, but he had created new momentum and hope for such change.

Gandhi remained in prison, but was able to carry on political activities. In February 1933 he announced the establishment of a new journal, which he called Harijan. *It would continue to be his principal mouthpiece for the rest of his life, though it was suspended several times. In March he was released from prison, and began a substantial change in interest and policy.*

The first issue of Harijan *appeared on February 11, 1933, five weeks after Gandhi's arrest. It contained two items which signal Gandhi's new emphasis on untouchability: the first is a message To the Reader, explaining justification and goals for the new publication, which include keeping all parties informed and nurturing support for the cause; the second consists of a statement of objection by Dr. Ambedkar on untouchability and caste, and Gandhi's reply.*

To the Reader

February 11, 1933

The English edition of 'Harijan' is being published by and for the Servants of Untouchables Society at my request and, therefore, in accordance with the views I have long held regarding reform Journals.

It is being published on the assumption that:

1. unfortunately, the Hindi edition cannot as yet serve the South and, probably, Bengal,

2. it is necessary for the people in the different provinces to know the progress of the reform from week to week in the provinces other than their own,

3. since the movement, though essentially Hindu, has a world wide significance and seeks the sympathy, if possible, of the whole of humanity, it is necessary to keep the world acquainted with its implications and progress.

If these assumptions are correct, 'Harijan' will supply a felt want and should, therefore, become self-supporting. If it does not, it must stop publication....

Ten thousand copies are being printed for the time being. Some copies will be sent free, either by way of compliment or exchange, but the list can only be limited. It is possible for you to extend it. I would like every English-knowing Harijan student and every untouchability worker to have a free copy on a certified application. That is possible only through the active co-operation of the reader who can afford to pay more than his own subscription.... By paying subscriptions for yourself or others you buy the right of, and recognize the duty of, serving the great cause in every legitimate manner possible for you. Thus you can become an active helper in spreading the message of 'Harijan' among those who are opposing the reform. This requires special qualifications. You need to have self-restraint. The opponents are in a state of rage just now.... They imagine much more than the reform means and, therefore, do not hesitate to ascribe motives to reformers....

If you will diligently study 'Harijan,' it will equip you for the delicate task.... I do not despair of even some opponents subscribing to 'Harijan.' I am an irrepressible optimist. I have no quarrel with the opponents. These pages will be written as much for them as for the reformers. If 'Harijan' stands for truth and if the reformers have patience, the opponents of today will be the reformers of to-morrow.

Fasting and the Removal of Untouchability

Dr. Ambedkar, himself an "untouchable," turned out to be one of Gandhi's most formidable opponents on the issues of untouchability. In February 1933, the following exchange of views took place.

Dr. Ambedkar and Caste

The following has just been received from Dr. Ambedkar:

> At the end of our conversation on Saturday last you asked me to send a message for insertion in the first issue of your new weekly *Harijan*. I feel I cannot give a message. For I believe it would be a most unwarranted presumption on my part to suppose that I have sufficient worth in the eyes of the Hindus which would make them treat any message from me with respect. I can only speak as man to man. As such it may be desirable that the Hindus should know my views on the momentous issue of Hindu social organization with which you have chosen to occupy yourself. I am, therefore,

sending you the accompanying statement for publication in your *Harijan*.

Statement:

The outcaste is a by-product of the caste system. There will be outcastes as long as there are castes. Nothing can emancipate the outcaste except the destruction of the caste system. Nothing can help to save Hindus and ensure their survival in the coming struggle except the purging of the Hindu faith of this odious and vicious dogma.

Gandhi's Reply:

Dr. Ambedkar is bitter. He has every reason to feel so. He has received a liberal education. He has more than the talents of the average educated Indian. Outside India he is received with honor and affection, but, in India, among Hindus, at every step he is reminded that he is one of the outcastes of Hindu society.... I would like him to feel that there are today thousands of caste Hindus who would listen to his message with the same respect and consideration that they would give to that of any other leader.... I would like him, too, to know that *Harijan* is not my weekly. So far as the proprietary rights are concerned, it belongs to the Servants of Untouchables Society and, therefore, I would like him to feel that it is as much his as of any other Hindu.

Three months later, still in prison, Gandhi began a major fast. He wanted to raise the nation's awareness of the untouchability issue and wanted orthodox Hindus to permit temple entry by untouchables. It was an unconditional fast, and it attracted wide attention from the press and from Gandhi's friends. In this public statement Gandhi explains the role of faith in his commitment to carrying out the fast.

His Will Be Done

May 6, 1933

General Smuts is reported to have made a pathetic appeal to me to desist from the impending fast. ... I have not yet received the telegram. But there seems to be no doubt about the authenticity of the report. ... Chakravarti Rajagopalachari, the keeper of my conscience, sends me a long telegram attacking the very basis of the fast.

Add to these the fervent personal appeal, strengthened by a copious flow of tears, of Devadas, my youngest son and valued comrade.

If these typical appeals have left me unmoved, the reader should have no difficulty in perceiving that there must be a force which has overpowered me and prevents me from responding to these and such other appeals.

Underlying them is undoubtedly a distrust in my claim that this fast is prompted by God. I do not suggest that they do not believe in my word. But they believe me to be under self-delusion—a prey to my own heated imagination made hotter by the suffocation produced by the cramping walls of a prison. I cannot deny the possibility of such a thing. But it can make no appeal to me whilst I believe to the contrary. I am a habitual prisoner. Prison walls have never been known to have warped my judgment or induced in me a habit of brooding. All my imprisonments have been periods of intense activity leaving me no time for brooding. I have undoubtedly brooded over the wrongs of Harijans. But such brooding has always resulted in definite action on my part. The action that I was contemplating on the day preceding that fateful night was certainly not any fast.

My claim to hear the voice of God is no new claim. Unfortunately there is no way that I know of proving the claim except through results. God will not be God if He allowed Himself to be an object of proof by His creatures. But he does give His willing slave the power to pass through the fieriest of ordeals. I have been a willing slave to this most exacting Master for more than half a century. His voice has been increasingly audible as years have rolled by. He has never forsaken me even in my darkest hour. He has saved me often against myself and left me not a vestige of independence. The greater the surrender to Him, the greater has been my joy.

I, therefore, feel confident that in the end these kindest of friends will recognize the correctness of the action I am about to take. And this whether

I die or live. God's ways are inscrutable. And who knows that He may not want my death during the fast to be more fruitful of beneficial results than my life? Surely it is highly depressing to think that a man's ability to serve dies with the dissolution of the body which for the moment he is inhabiting. Who doubts that the spirits of Ramkrishna and Dayanand, Vivekanand and Ramtirth[61] are to-day working in our midst? It may be that they are more potent to-day than when they were in our midst in the flesh. It is not true that 'the good that men do is oft buried with them.' We burn the evil that men do with their mortal remains. We treasure the memory of the good they do, and distance only magnifies it.

And why should exaggerated importance be given to the services of one single person, however good or able he may be? The cause of Harijans is God's cause. He will throw up men and women as they may be required to do His will.

I, therefore, invite General Smuts and all other friends to believe with me that I am not acting under hallucination and beseech them to send up their prayer to the Almighty that He may give me the strength to pass safely through the ordeal. I feel sure that, if I am wanted on this earth yet for a while for any service whatsoever, He will spare me notwithstanding the fears of medical friends.

M. K. Gandhi

This statement was issued in The Bombay Chronicle *at noon on the day that Gandhi had commenced his fast:*

Statement Explaining Object of Fast

May 8, 1933

Every day brings me fresh justification for the ordeal that God the Truth has sent me. The discoveries I am making would have paralysed me, but for the fast. Whatever it may mean for the cause, it will certainly be my saving. Whether I survive the fast or not, is a matter of little moment. Without it I

61. Ramkrishna and Dayanand, Vivekanand and Ramtirth: famous Hindu teachers and philosophers

would, in all probability, have been useless for further service of Harijans, and for that matter, any other service.

Those friends who have sent me urgent wires dissuading me from the step will, I hope, appreciate the fact that for a person built as I am, such fasts are indispensable. This I say apart from my claim, by which I stand, that it was God's call.

The senders of wires will forgive me for not sending individual acknowledgments. The pressure upon my time has been so great that it has been physically impossible for me to cope with all wires that poured in upon me.

Now that the fast will begin within two hours of writing this, I invite all friends and well-wishers to pray for strength for enabling me to go through the ordeal without weakening. I confess that I have no strength except what God may give me. That He has never failed me hitherto gives me the confidence that He will not fail me now.

A telegram was received by me from a Harijan Association that my fast was unnecessary, as the Harijans do not stand in need of assistance from the caste Hindus. From its own standpoint, the Association is right. Only it should be clearly understood that the fast is taken not to oblige the Harijans, but for purification of self and associates.

Harijan service is a duty the caste Hindus owe to themselves. It is a part of the penance they must do for the wrongs they have done to their own kith and kin. I can well understand the indignant repudiation by some of the Harijans. Let me hope that it is not yet too late for the vast majority to accept the penance. The numerous messages I have received from them leave no room for doubting such an acceptance.

Sanatanist[62] Hindus scent further coercion in this fast. When they realize that it cannot be broken before its period, even if every temple was opened and untouchability removed from the heart, they will perhaps admit that it cannot be regarded as in any way coercive. The fast is intended to remove bitterness, to purify hearts and to make it clear that the movement is wholly moral, to be prosecuted by wholly moral persons. May God bless the ordeal and fulfill its purpose.

---

62. Sanatanist: a sect which believed in preserving traditional forms of Hindu practice

Comments on the Fast

Of the comments and appeals which Gandhi receives, four are included below, which he refers to. They came from very different sources, and provide some sense of the impact of Gandhi's actions. The following telegram came from Gandhi's opponent in South Africa, General Smuts, who had become Gandhi's friend and who had met with Gandhi in London.

From General Jan Christiaan Smuts

May 6, 1933

May I appeal to you most earnestly to delay your announced fast? Your work for removal of untouchability has already achieved a measure of success which exceeds highest expectations. With patience you may yet carry complete accomplishment of the greatest reform of our time. Moreover, India stands on the threshold of a new period which makes your wise guidance in future more essential than ever before. Endangering your life might lead to a dreadful calamity and an irreparable setback at the most critical moment. I appeal for old friendship's sake and for the great causes you have championed so successfully.

The following telegram is from Rabindranath Tagore (1861–1941), the great poet of India and recipient of the Nobel Prize for Literature in 1913, whose ashram, Shantiniketan, "The House of Peace," Gandhi had visited on his return from South Africa.

Rabindranath Tagore

Glen Eden, Darjeeling
May 11, 1933

Dear Mahatmaji,

I am trying clearly to find out the meaning contained in this last message of yours which is before the world today. In every important act of his life Buddha preached limitless love for all creatures. Christ said "Love your enemies," and that teaching of his found its final expression in the words of forgiveness he uttered for those who killed him. As far as I can understand, the fast that you have started carries in it the idea of expiation for the sins of your countrymen. But I ask to be excused when I say that the expiation can truly and heroically be done only by daily endeavours for the sake of those unfortunate beings who do not know what they do. The fasting, which has no direct action upon the conduct of misdoers and which may abruptly terminate one's power further to serve those who need help, cannot be universally accepted, and therefore it is all the more unacceptable for any individual who has the responsibility to represent humanity.

The logical consequence of your example, if followed, will be an elimination of all noble souls from the morally feeble and downtrodden multitude to sink into the fathomless depth of ignorance and iniquity. You have no right to say that this process of penance can only be efficacious through your own individual endeavour and for others it has no meaning. If that were true you ought to have performed it in absolute secrecy as a special mystic rite which only claims its one sacrifice beginning and ending in yourself. You ask others to actively devote their energy to extirpate the evil which smothers our national life and enjoin only upon yourself an extreme form of sacrifice which is of a passive character. For lesser men than yourself it opens up an easy and futile path of duty by urging them to take a plunge into a dark abyss of self-mortification. You cannot blame them if they follow you in this special method of purification of their country, for all messages must be universal in their application, and if not they should never be expressed at all.

The suffering that has been caused to me by the vow you have taken has compelled me to write you thus—for I cannot bear the sight of a sublimely noble career journeying towards a finality which, to my mind, lacks a perfectly satisfying justification. And once again I appeal to you for the sake of the dignity of our nation, which is truly impersonated in you, and for the sake of the millions of my countrymen who need your living touch and help, to desist from any act that you think is good only for you and not for the rest of humanity.

With the deepest pain and love,

Yours,
(Sr) Rabindranath Tagore

Another telegram was from Romain Rolland, Gandhi's early biographer, whom Gandhi had visited in Switzerland as he was returning to India in 1931. His sense in 1933 of the world war which would begin six years later is particularly interesting.

From Romain Rolland, "The Meaning of the Fast"

May 27, 1933

We are with you in these grave days when your life is once again at stake. We send forth our fervent prayers that the hardness of heart of those of your people who obstruct the great work of national reparation to the untouchables gives way; that they should tremble to assume before history the execrable responsibility of having caused your death. They will, in the memory of all men of the future, always carry the mark on their forehead.

But permit me to attach to your sacrifice a larger meaning yet than that for the cause of the untouchables. In these tragic times, when the whole world is given over to the most atrocious violence—on the eve of the world wars which in their amplitude and cruelty will overshadow all those of the past—when the whole of humanity is divided between the oppressors and the oppressed—and when the latter, ground down by their sufferings and injustice, as if made drunk by the violence which makes martyrs of them see before them no help except in violence—your immolation before the Goddess of Justice, who is all love and without violence, acquires a universal and sacred value—like the Cross.

If the Cross has not—alas—saved the world, it has shown the world the way to save itself: it has illumined with its light the night of millions of unfortunates.

The fourth was not a message to Gandhi, but a comment from an Indian Christian in support of the fast. It was published first in the Guardian, *and reprinted in* Harijan.

S. K. George ("Is Satyagraha Christian?")

May 27, 1933

... If the charge of deliberate courting of suffering and death is to be brought against the Mahatma's latest act, it ought with equal force to be leveled against his whole method of Satyagraha. For fasting unto death in obedience to an inner conviction is, as Gandhiji himself says, only the final form, the Crown of Satyagraha. The element of deliberate choice, of going out to face danger in order to bring moral pressure on the object of it, is present in all manifestations of Satyagraha, from the picketing of a foreign cloth shop up to the starving of oneself to death. But is not that the very element of newness in it, that which it adds to the practice of Christianity and the other religions which have preached the conquest of evil by love? Satyagraha seems to reduce to a system the art of grappling with evil, the science of aggressive love attacking evil in its strongholds and dragging it out into the open for a life and death struggle. The Cross of Christ is the supreme, perfect, historic example of such assault and victory of love over evil. But, alas, Christianity has made of it a creed, a doctrine, a belief in which is to secure a heaven of comfort and security. It was necessary to bring it back from the realm of creed and dogma and set it up again as a working principle of life, still mighty to overthrow entrenched evil and applicable to the problems of every-day life. That is what has been achieved by one who does not profess himself a Christian but in whom the central Christian principle of the Cross has again incarnated itself....

... Another element of safety in the practice of Satyagraha is its demand of the inner guiding voice of God. Satyagraha is only to be undertaken at the call of God. He it is "who alone canst order the unruly wills and affections of sinful men" and who alone can, therefore, make the suffering of the innocent change the heart of the indifferent.... Surely, Satyagraha can be, and ought to be, used as a Christian weapon in the fight for truth and justice in society and in the individual, to which the Christian is committed by his profession. Christians ought, therefore, to be profoundly thankful to the Mahatma for his demonstration of the potency and practicability of the method of the cross and to ponder over the significance of his latest offering of love which has compelled the attention of the world. "Greater love hath no man than this: that a man lay down his life for his friends."

Gandhi persisted in carrying out his twenty-one-day fast, and survived it. Two months later he gave a further explanation of what he had done, and explained more fully the "Voice" which he felt was guiding him.

All About the Fast

July 8, 1933

... The first question that has puzzled many is about the Voice of God. What was it? What did I hear? Was there any person I saw? If not, how was the Voice conveyed to me? These are pertinent questions.

For me the Voice of God, of Conscience, of Truth or the Inner Voice or 'the still small Voice' mean one and the same thing. I saw no form. I have never tried, for I have always believed God to be without form. But what I did hear was like a Voice from afar and yet quite near. It was as unmistakable as some human voice definitely speaking to me, and irresistible. I was not dreaming at the time I heard the Voice. The hearing of the Voice was preceded by a terrific struggle within me. Suddenly the Voice came upon me. I listened, made certain that it was the Voice, and the struggle ceased. I was calm. The determination was made accordingly, the date and the hour of the fast were fixed. Joy came over me. This was between 11 and 12 midnight. I felt refreshed and began to write the note about it which the reader must have seen.

Could I give any further evidence that it was truly the Voice that I heard and that it was not an echo of my own heated imagination? I have no further evidence to convince the skeptic. He is free to say that it was all self delusion or hallucination. It may well have been so. I can offer no proof to the contrary. But I can say this—that not the unanimous verdict of the whole world against me could shake me from the belief that what I heard was the true Voice of God.

But some think that God Himself is a creation of our own imagination. If that view holds good, then nothing is real, everything is of our own imagination. Even so, whilst my imagination dominates me, I can only act under its spell. Realest things are only relatively so. For me the Voice was more real than my own existence. It has never failed me, and for that matter, anyone else.

And everyone who wills can hear the Voice. It is within everyone. But like everything else, it requires previous and definite preparation. …

The fast was an uninterrupted twenty-one days' prayer whose effect I can feel even now. I know now more fully than ever that there is no prayer without fasting, be the latter ever so little. And this fasting relates not merely to the palate, but all the senses and organs. Complete absorption in prayer must mean complete exclusion of physical activities till prayer possesses the whole of our being and we rise superior to, and are completely detached from, all physical functions. That state can only be reached after continual and voluntary crucifixion of the flesh. Thus all fasting, if it is a spiritual act, is an intense prayer or a preparation for it. It is a yearning of the soul to merge in the divine essence. My last fast was intended to be such a preparation. How far I have succeeded, how far I am in tune with the Infinite, I do not know. But I do know that the fast has made the passion for such a state intenser than ever. …

The work of removal of untouchability is not merely a social or economic reform whose extent can be measured by so much social amenities or economic relief provided in so much time. Its goal is to touch the hearts of the millions of Hindus who honestly believe in the present day untouchability as a God-made institution, as old as the human race itself. This, it will be admitted, is a task infinitely higher than mere social and economic reform. Its accomplishment undoubtedly includes all these and much more. For it means nothing short of a complete revolution in the Hindu thought and the disappearance of the horrible and terrible doctrine of inborn inequality and high-and-lowness, which has poisoned Hinduism and is slowly undermining its existence. Such a change can only be brought about by an appeal to the highest in man. And I am more than ever convinced that that appeal can be made effective only by self-purification, i.e., by fasting conceived as the deepest prayer coming from a lacerated heart. …

In the next writing, Gandhi moved from the mystical and religious approach to the problem of untouchability to a graphic account of the actual condition of some Harijans.

A "Double Hell"

November 1, 1933

A Harijan servant in Orissa gives me a graphic description of his visit to some Harijan quarters in Balasore District, near Bhadrak:

> This year, as you know, there was too much rain in these parts. Therefore, when we neared the Harijan quarters, we found it surrounded by water on all sides. The stench coming from that water was unbearable. Naturally, when we waded through it, we found the quarter sodden, foul-smelling and too damp for human habitation. The grass roofs were all leaking and water was dripping from them, for we had gone just after the rains. The walls of these huts could not have been more than 4,' the surface no more than 7' x 5.' In the hut opposite, there was an apology for a verandah, perhaps a foot and a half wide. Bones and pieces of rotting leather were strewn on the floor. Wherever you set your foot, it would go down knee-deep. If the spirit of service did not possess us, we certainly would have turned away from the place which one would not use even for cattle. You have described one of the quarters as a 'hell upon earth.' And if what you described was a hell, I have no doubt that, if you could see this quarter as we have seen it, you would call it a double hell. We had gone with a view to cleaning this quarter. There was not much that lent itself to cleaning here, but when we began it, the Harijans said: 'Bapu,[63] why have you come to us low people?' When we spoke to the owner of the house about the verandah and suggested that he ought not to allow stinking leather to remain on it, he said: 'Bapu, this is my wealth. I have no other place to store it. You are the first people to come to us about cleanliness and other things, but what is the use of our doing anything? We have to eke out our existence

63. Bapu: literally, "father" used as a term of endearment; Gandhi's wife Kasturba is similarly called Ba, "mother."

> as best we may.' To stay for any length of time in this place was impossible. One of us was so overcome by the stink that on reaching our abode he fell ill and remained in bed for 24 hours before he could think of taking any food. Nausea had overtaken him. This quarter that I have described to you is not very far from the Chandan Bazar of Bhadrak. The place is called Esopir. It has about 15 houses with a population of 65. Not far from it are to be found very substantial kottis[64] belonging to merchants.

Is it any wonder that we have malaria, plague, and cholera rampant in our midst? It is impossible to avoid these diseases so long as we neglect these useful members of society, consign them to the dirtiest places and, because of the monster of untouchability, we would not teach them to do their work in a proper and efficient manner. I suggest to workers all over the country that they must concentrate their effort upon the plague spots which they visit. Let us not be baffled by the vastness of the problem. Things will right themselves if everyone will attend to the work that comes his way. I would, therefore, advise the workers of Bhadrak to go to the merchants, make out a simple plan of improvement, present them with a budget, level up the ground, put up plinths[65] and rebuild the fifteen houses. It cannot be a heavy budget and I doubt not that by sufficient importunity they will be able to raise a fund to reduce that plan to execution. The donors will find that the donations are a sound investment in a health-promoting project. It would be like putting their courtyards in order.

M. K. Gandhi

Continuing the Harijan effort, Gandhi tried various ways of reaching people. For months he traveled by train, but in this article he explains his reasons for doing some of his travelling on foot. The article gives us a picture of how Gandhi sees the campaign he is carrying out, its personal nature, and its religious focus.

64. kottis: cottages or homes

65. plinth: a square block serving as a base

Statement to the Press ("Shall it be on Foot?")

May 11, 1934

The idea is growing on me that I should finish the balance of the Harijan tour by walking as far as it may be possible.... I would love to demonstrate to them in every way I can that the movement is essentially religious in conception and execution. If the motive is religious, so is the end sought. I am anxious too to show that it does not depend for its spread upon swift locomotion. A suggestion that I should use the aeroplane was dismissed as soon as it was made. Nor need anyone run away with the idea that the tour has been undertaken for the sole purpose of collecting funds.... It is likely that if my message comes from the heart, it will travel faster on foot than by rail or motor. And then I am tired of the terrific noises. Though they are an expression of people's affection and joy at seeing me, they jar on my nerves, which have now become too weak to bear them. I am equally tired of the hustling that has become my daily lot. The pressing towards me of vast crowds and the frantic efforts of volunteers to protect me from those crowds are proving too much for my weak body....

I have made little lasting impression in spite of having strongly disapproved of the shouts, the pressings and the touching of feet. I do produce a local impression when I succeed in being heard. This opportunity cannot occur to me often when I have to rush through space as I have been doing and have to take, during the day, three places far apart from one another. For the essential truth of the message to soak into the people, it has to be delivered to silent and listening crowds. Religious truth, or for that matter any truth, requires a calm and meditative atmosphere for its percolation....

This brief editorial is a concise summary of Gandhi's radical view of an ideal village-centered economy. He is too much of a realist to believe that such an economy can be achieved in the near future, but he still sees it as an objective worth working for. It is interesting to note that he grounds his ideas in both the Bhagavad-Gita and the Bible.

Duty of Bread Labour

June 29, 1935

Brahma created his people with the duty of sacrifice laid upon them and said: "By this do you flourish. Let it be the fulfiller of all your desires. He who eats without performing this sacrifice eats stolen bread."

Thus says the Gita. "Earn thy bread by the sweat of thy brow," says the Bible. Sacrifices may be of many kinds. One of them may well be bread labour. If all laboured for their bread and no more, then there would be enough food and enough leisure for all. Then there would be no cry of overpopulation, no disease, and no such misery as we see around.

Such labour will be the highest form of a sacrifice. Men will no doubt do many other things either through their bodies or through their minds, but all this will be labour of love, for the common good. There will then be no rich and no poor, none high and none low, no touchable and no untouchable.

This may be an unattainable ideal. But we need not, therefore, cease to strive for it. Even if without fulfilling the whole law of sacrifice, that is, the law of our being, we performed physical labour enough for our daily bread, we should go a long way towards the ideal.

If we did so, our wants would be minimized, our food would be simple. We should then eat to live, not live to eat. Let anyone who doubts the accuracy of this proposition try to sweat for his bread. He will derive the greatest relish from the productions of his labour, improve his health and discover that many things he took were superfluities.

May not men earn their bread by intellectual labour? No. The needs of the body must be supplied by the body. "Render unto Caesar that which is Caesar's" perhaps applies here as well.

Mere mental, that is, intellectual labour is for the soul and is its own satisfaction. It should never demand payment. In the ideal State, doctors, lawyers and the like will work solely for the benefit of society, not for self. Obedience to the law of bread labour will bring about a silent revolution in the structure of society. Man's triumph will consist in substituting the struggle for existence by the struggle for mutual service. The law of the brute will be replaced by the law of man.

Return to the villages means a definite voluntary recognition of the duty of bread labour and all it connotes. But says the critic, "millions of

India's children are today living in the villages and yet they are living a life of semi-starvation." This, alas, is but too true. Fortunately we know that theirs is not voluntary obedience. They would perhaps shirk body labour if they could, and even rush to the nearest city if they could be accommodated in it. Compulsory obedience to a master is state of slavery; willing obedience to one's father is the glory of sonship. Similarly compulsory obedience to the law of bread labour breeds poverty, disease and discontent. It is a state of slavery. Willing obedience to it must bring contentment and health. And it is health which is real wealth, not pieces of silver and gold. The Village Industries Association is an experiment in willing bread labour.

But the issues of war and peace did not occupy Gandhi's whole attention. Several months later in a discussion with Maurice Frydman he went back to economic issues, such as the relation of physical comforts and spirituality, and his focus on the importance of village-based independence. Frydman was a Polish engineer who was interested in village reconstruction. He visited Gandhi at Wardha, and later developed a very simple spindle, which could be made by a village carpenter, and would produce yarn at a rate comparable to that of the spinning wheel. Frydman also adopted the Indian name of Bharatanand.

A Discussion with Maurice Frydman

[On or before August 25, 1935]

[Frydman] inquired if Gandhiji's aim was just humanitarian in sitting down in the village, just serving the villagers as best he could.

[Gandhi replied:] I am here to serve no one else but myself, to find my own self-realization through the service of these village folk. Man's ultimate aim is the realization of God, and all his activities, social, political, religious, have to be guided by the ultimate aim of the vision of God. The immediate service of all human beings becomes a necessary part of the endeavour simply because the only way to find God is to see Him in His creation and be one with it. This can only be done by service of all. And this cannot be done except through one's country. I am part and parcel of the whole, and I cannot find Him apart from the rest of humanity. My countrymen are my nearest neighbours. They have become so helpless, so resourceless, so inert that I must concentrate on serving them. If I could persuade myself that I should find Him in a Himalayan cave, I would proceed there immediately. But I know that I cannot find Him apart from humanity.

[Frydman:] But some comforts may be necessary even for man's spiritual advancement. One could not advance himself by identifying himself with the discomfort and squalour of the villager?

[Gandhi:] A certain degree of physical harmony and comfort is necessary, but above a certain level it becomes a hindrance instead of help. Therefore the ideal of creating an unlimited number of wants and satisfying them seems to be a delusion and a snare. The satisfaction of one's physical needs, even the intellectual needs of one's narrow self, must meet at a certain point a dead stop, before it degenerates into physical and intellectual voluptuousness. A man must arrange his physical and cultural circumstances so that they do not hinder him in his service of humanity, on which all his energies should be concentrated.

[Frydman:] What then was the secret of your concentration on the village?

[Gandhi:] I have been saying that if untouchability stays, Hinduism goes; even so I would say that if the village perishes, India will perish too. It will be no more India. Her own mission in the world will get lost. The revival of the village is possible only when it is no more exploited. Industrialization on a mass scale will necessarily lead to passive or active exploitation of the villagers as the problems of competition and marketing come in. Therefore we have to concentrate on the village being self-contained, manufacturing mainly for use. Provided this character of the village industry is maintained, there would be no objection to villagers using even the modern machines and tools that they can make and can afford to use. Only they should not be used as a means of exploitation of others.

But the world was already moving toward crisis, and in October 1935, Gandhi turns again to the theme of nonviolence as Mussolini launches his attack on Abyssinia in what is sometimes seen as the opening action leading to World War II. Gandhi had had an unsatisfactory interview with Mussolini on his return from the London Round Table. The following is an extraordinary statement of non-violent policy in the midst of a war.

The Greatest Force

October 12, 1935

Non-violence is at the root of every one of my activities and therefore also of the three public activities on which I am just now visibly concentrating all my energy. These are untouchability, khadi, and village regeneration in general. Hindu-Muslim unity is my fourth love. But so far as any visible manifestation is concerned, I have owned defeat on that score. Let the public, however, not assume there from that I am inactive. If not during my lifetime, I know that after my death both Hindus and Mussalmans will bear witness that I had never ceased to yearn after communal peace.

Non-violence to be a creed has to be all-pervasive. I cannot be non-violent about one activity of mine and violent about others. That would be a policy, not a life-force. That being so, I cannot be indifferent about the war that Italy is now waging against Abyssinia. But I have resisted most pressing invitation to express my opinion and give a lead to the country. ... If India had as a nation imbibed the creed of non-violence, corporate or national, I should have had no hesitation in giving a lead. But in spite of a certain hold I have on the millions of this country, I know the very grave and glaring limitation of that hold. India had an unbroken tradition of non-violence from times immemorial. But at no time in her ancient history, as far as I know it, has it had complete non-violence in action pervading the whole land. Nevertheless, it is my unshakable belief that her destiny is to deliver the message of non-violence to mankind. It may take ages to come to fruition. But so far as I can judge, no other country will precede her in the fulfillment of that mission.

Be that as it may, it is seasonable to contemplate the implications of that matchless force. Three concrete questions were, the other day, incidentally asked by friends:

1. What could ill-armed Abyssinia do against well-armed Italy, if she were non-violent?

2. What could England, the greatest and the most powerful member of the League, do against determined Italy, if she (England) were non-violent in your sense of the term?

3. What could India do, if she suddenly became non-violent in your sense of the term?

Before I answer the questions let me lay down five simple axioms of non-violence as I know it.

1. Non-violence implies as complete self purification as is humanly possible.

2. Man for man the strength of non-violence is in exact proportion to the ability, not the will, of the non-violent person to inflict violence.

3. Non-violence is without exception superior to violence, i.e., the power at the disposal of a non-violent person is always greater than he would have if he was violent.

4. There is no such thing as defeat in non-violence. The end of violence is surest defeat.

5. The ultimate end of non-violence is surest victory—if such a term may be used of non-violence. In reality where there is no sense of defeat, there is no sense of victory.

The foregoing questions may be answered in the light of these axioms.

1. If Abyssinia were non-violent, she would have no arms, would want none. She would make no appeal to the League [of Nations] or any other power for armed intervention. She would never give any cause for complaint. And Italy would find nothing to conquer if Abyssinians would not offer armed resistance, nor would they give co-operation willing or forced. Italian occupation in that case would mean that of the land without its people. That, however, is not Italy's exact object. She seeks submission of the people of a beautiful land.

2. If Englishmen were as a nation to become non-violent at heart, they would shed imperialism, they would give up the use of arms. The moral force generated by such an act of renunciation would stagger Italy into willing surrender of her designs. England would then be a living embodiment of the axioms I have laid down. The effect of such conversion would mean the greatest miracle of all ages. And yet if non-violence is not an idle dream, some such thing has some day to come to pass somewhere. I live in that faith.

3. The last question may be answered thus. As I have said, India as a nation is not non-violent in the full sense of the term. Neither has she any capacity for offering violence—not because she has no arms. Physical possession of arms is the least necessity of the brave. Her non-violence is that of the weak. She betrays her weakness in many of her daily acts. She appears before the world today as a decaying nation. I mean here not in the mere political sense but essentially in the non-violent, moral sense. She lacks the ability to offer physical resistance. She has no consciousness of strength. She is conscious only of her weakness. If she were otherwise, there would be no communal problems, nor political. If she were non-violent in the consciousness of her strength, Englishmen would lose their role of distrustful conquerors. We may talk politically as we like and often legitimately blame the English rulers. But if we, as Indians, could but for a moment visualize ourselves as a strong people disdaining to strike, we should cease to fear Englishmen whether as soldiers, traders or administrators, and they to distrust us. Therefore if we became truly non-violent we should carry Englishmen with us in all we might do. In other words, we being millions would be the greatest moral force in the world, and Italy would listen to our friendly word. …

Till my eyes of geometrical understanding had been opened, my brain was swimming, as I read and re-read the twelve axioms of Euclid. After the opening of my eyes geometry seemed to be the easiest science to learn. Much more so is the case with non-violence. It is a matter of faith and experience, not of argument beyond a point. So long as the world refuses to believe, she must await a miracle, i.e., an ocular demonstration of non-violence on a mass scale. They say this is against human nature—non-violence is only for the individual. If so, where is the difference in kind between man and beast?

Gandhi is struggling between his wish to spend all his time on village work, and the demands of friends and associates who keep coming to see him. This statement, which was written before September 2, 1936, gives the reader an idea of what he is trying to do, and how he feels about it.

Talk with Kumarappa[66]

[Before September 2, 1936]

... I long to wander among the villages around us rather than go to Wardha where so many friends are coming and I may have to go. But I feel it a wrench to be torn from my work.... I have two or three engagements which I accepted long ago and I shall have to keep them, though I would love to find some excuse to put them off or avoid them. I would like to walk out every morning to the villages in our neighbourhood. I am doing practically little physical work now, and I am longing to do it. We have taken a couple of cows and are trying the experiment of making our own ghee.[67] Now I should like to look after the cow myself, look after her food and her general upkeep. My idea is to show these villagers that a cow can easily pay for her feed and the charges of her upkeep. Then look at the number of ailments these villagers suffer from, and how they will try all kinds of quack remedies but will not do the simplest things they must do.

66. Bharatan Kumarappa is the younger brother of J.C. Kumarappa, an economist and a Christian, educated at Columbia University, and a close associate of Gandhi (*CWMG-CD* 80:272n2; Rajmohan Gandhi 316).

67. ghee: clarified butter

All this is slow work.... Our acid test is: Have we organized any single village according to our programme? Have we introduced food reform there? Are their roads and their lanes clean and perfect? Have we revived any industries? Have we tackled the problem of drink and vice? If we could do this successfully even in one village, I should think we had achieved a good deal. From individuals you may get a response but I should not call it making headway. Making headway is touching one whole village. Jajuji was wondering if we might not have a wider scheme. No, we cannot have it. It is not one item of work like hand-spinning for instance. It is whole village-work, and today our work centers round three or four things I have mentioned. It may centre round thirty things some day, but not today.

Excerpts from this article, which appeared in Harijan, *give a vivid picture of Gandhi's personal approach to the village work to which he is now dedicating himself. He has chosen Wardha as the site of Segaon, a new ashram, and wants to live in the village, suffer with the villagers, and teach them himself. But he has been ill, and has sought medical attention that is beyond the limited capacity of the villages to provide.*

Of My Recent Illness

September 19, 1936

I would not tax the reader about my recent malaria fever except for the fact that friends are involved in the decision I have prayerfully made and which I hope God will let me fulfill.

It went against the grain for me, a confirmed believer in nature-cure methods, to go to Wardha and seek admission to the hospital. Left entirely to myself, I would have treated myself in accordance with nature-cure methods as far as possible. But I could not do so without offending the friends who happened to be near me at the time. I knew that Jamnalalji[68] too had a special responsibility, in that I had settled in a village near Wardha, his

68. Jamnalal Bajaj (1884–1942), a businessman and industrialist from Wardha, was one of Gandhi's closest associates and supporters. Gandhi treated him as an adopted son and felt a significant emotional blow when Bajaj died in 1942 (Rajmohan Gandhi 203, 447).

permanent place of residence. With the choice of the village he has had nothing to do. It was entirely Mirabehn's and it was made because Segaon was predominantly a Harijan village and far enough from Wardha and yet not too far. I was drawn to the village in accordance with a certain declaration I had made when Mirabehn went to Segaon.... Having gone to Segaon it was my intention not to stir out of it for ... one year. Unfortunately there are obligations undertaken before the decision to settle in Segaon, which I shall have to fulfill and which will disturb the unbroken year's stay. I urge friends, therefore, not to make further inroads upon the period.... I set the greatest value upon the village problem.... India lives in her villages, not in her cities. I am supposed to guide and direct the village industries movement to which at Bombay an autonomous existence was given by the Congress [in October 1934]. I am incapable of guiding any movement in which I do not plunge myself actively and directly. Maganwadi, though a village, being a large village, was not good enough.... I needed to be in a real village presenting the problems that face one in generality [sic] of villages. Segaon is one such village.

If then I may not leave Segaon in order not to interrupt my instruction and first-hand experience, I may not also leave it for health reasons. Segaon like most villages has its full share of malaria and other diseases which villagers suffer from. Of its population of 600 there is hardly anyone who has not suffered from malaria or dysentery.... The simple remedies at our disposal with dietetic control have served their purpose effectively. The villagers do not go to hospitals, they cannot even go to dispensaries. They usually resort to village quacks or incantations and drag on their weary existence. I claim to have some workable knowledge of common ailments. I have successfully treated myself often enough without the assistance of medical friends though they have been ever ready to help me in my need. If I were not a 'Mahatma,' so-called, no one would have known anything of the recent attack of malaria. I rarely have fever. The last attack I had was nearly 12 years ago and I had treated myself. There is all the greater reason for me now, if I have another attack of malaria, or another ailment, not to stir out of Segaon.... One like myself struggling to become a humble village servant surely ought to be satisfied with remedies easily accessible to villages. By leaving my village in search of health or the like I deny myself the opportunity of knowing what village life can be when one's health is in peril.

My malaria has quickened my resolve to study the problem of making Segaon malaria-proof. All round me the fields are water-logged. The crops are rotting. The ground is unwalkable unless you are content to wade through knee-deep mud. Fortunately a pukka[69] road was built for my convenience through Jamnalalji's fields which keeps Segaon somewhat accessible to people from Wardha. The road has proved a great convenience for man and beast. If I had listened to friend's advice to postpone settling in Segaon till after the rains, I would have missed the rich experiences I have gained during the heavy rains of the past two months. Everything I have seen hitherto therefore convinces me that, if I am to make any approach to the village life, I must persevere in my resolve not to desert it in the hour of danger to life or limb. And I ask all the friends to help me in carrying out the resolve and pray with me that God may give me the strength to do so.

These excerpts give us a more detailed picture of Gandhi's dedication to Segaon and some of his ideas on education, which like his ideas on economics, center on the village. He is speaking to Gujaratis[70] who know him and his earlier ashram near Ahmedabad, and he is introducing them to Segaon and conditions in other parts of India.

Excerpts from Speech at Gujarati Sahitya Parishad[71]

October 31, 1936

...I live in Segaon today where in a population of 600 a little over ten are literate.... Of the ten or more who can read, there are scarcely three or four who can understand what they read, and among the women there is not one who is literate... thought of setting up a little library for them. The books had to be of course within their understanding, and so I begged a dozen school books from two or three girls who had no use for them.

69. pukka: splendid, first-class

70. Gujaratis: members of the state of Gujarat where Gandhi was born and grew up

71. The Gujarati Sahitya Parishad, literally "Gujarati Literary Conference" was established in 1905, and Gandhi served as its president in 1936 (Usha Thakkar, Mani Bhavan Gandhi Sangrahalaya, correspondence with editors).

I could make you laugh a great deal if I spoke to you about the authors of those worthless text-books and I could talk about them for hours but we don't have the time.

The place is a part of Maharashtra. There is not as much illiteracy as in Gujarat, but Segaon is almost entirely illiterate. I have with me a young man who is an LLB but who has forgotten all his law and cast in his lot with me. He is from Gujarat but knows some Marathi. He goes to the village and reads to those who come to him from these books whatever they can follow and digest. He takes a newspaper or two with him. But how is he to make them follow our newspapers? What do they know of Spain and of Russia? What do they know of geography? The place which houses these books worth three and a half rupees is such that one cannot sit under the roof during the monsoon. If anyone applied a matchstick, it would go up in flames. It was really Mirabehn's hut… But in that hut belonging to Mirabehn we set up a library.…

I could speak on to you for hours telling you what I want. I want art and literature that can speak to the millions. I have given you an outline of the picture. You will fill in the details. I have said my say. My heart is weeping at the present moment, but time has made it hard enough not to break even when there are occasions for it. As I think of Segaon and its skeletons—[here he did break down]—as I think of Segaon and its folk, I can't help saying that our literature is a miserable affair. Principal Anandshankar Dhruva sent me a list of a hundred books, but none of them would do for them. What am I to place before them? And their women! Is there any relation, I wonder, between them and the Ahmedabad ladies I see in front of me? The Segaon women know no literature. They cannot even repeat the Ramadhun[72] with me. They simply know how to drudge and slave away. Reckless of sun or rain, of snakes or scorpions, they fetch water, they cut grass and hew wood, and look upon me as their benefactor if I give them work and a few coppers. … I am no speaker, neither is the pen my profession. I have written what I have because I could not help it, and at one time I was dumb, so much so that my friends used to call me a dunce, until I went to the courts where too it was with difficulty that I opened my lips. It is not my business to speak or to write. My business is to live amongst them and show them how to live. The

72. Ramadhun: devotional song of lord Rama

key to swaraj is not in the cities but in the villages, and so I have settled in a village—a village, too, which I did not go seeking, but which came to me.

In a speech a few days later, Gandhi expands on the sort of books and education he wishes would be available to the villagers.

Speech at the Concluding Session of the Twelfth Gujarati Sahitya Parishad

Ahmedabad

... It is not that I do not like to read good essays. I have some interests which I cannot satisfy. A good many of these have become extinguished, but those that are still alive will keep showing up on every occasion so long as I have not been able to see God. Anandshankarbhai told me that a poetry symposium was held here and even young men participated fully. I had wished to go to the lecture on the archaeological work in Indore. But I neither went to the lecture nor attended the poetry symposium. What can it be but generosity on your part that you have put up with all these failings of mine?

On hearing about the donations for prizes, I was reminded of Carnegie who endowed a large library in Scotland. Professors in Scotland told him: 'If you want to make a donation, why insist on a library? You know about business; what can you know of these matters?' I, too, would tell our philanthropists that if they want to make sure that their money would be well spent they should give us donations without attaching any conditions. ...

I live in a village and so I can acquaint you with my hunger as a villager. While doing my matriculation I read a book on astronomy, but no one then asked me to look at the sky. Kakasaheb is a man of keen interests. In Yeravda jail, he used to gaze at the stars every night. I wondered what he could be gazing at. But after his release I too asked for books on the subject. I wanted a Gujarati book and I even found one although worthless. But how could that appease my hunger? Could we not give to our villagers a book on astronomy which they could understand?

But not to speak of astronomy, do we even have books on geography which they could understand? The fact is that we have not paid any attention to the villagers. Although we are dependent upon them for our food and clothing, we behave as if we were their masters. We have given no thought whatsoever to their requirements. Is there any other country which is so impoverished that it carries on its business in a foreign language while ignoring its own? It is for this very reason that our country continues to be poor and our language is in a state of widowhood. There is not a single book in French or German, which soon after its publication is not translated into English. Abridged versions of the best classics are produced in large numbers for children. Have we anything like that in Gujarati? If that were the case, I would bless it.

I had wanted to introduce a resolution on this subject, but now I shall be content with merely making the suggestion. I entreat our writers to begin writing for our dumb masses rather than for our city-dwellers. I am the self-appointed representative of that dumb public. On their behalf, I ask you to take a plunge into that field. You may be writing entertaining stories but these are not going to make any impression upon their minds. We have a school for village workers. I asked its teacher to study the tools used in a craft before teaching it, to understand how a basala[73] is made. If you wish to develop your mind, you should study village implements, understand their good points and bad points and then write about them. Those whose minds are fresh will find new things to see and to learn in villages. It is not true that your mental development becomes stunted when you go to the villages. My reply to those who say this would be that they must have gone there with close minds. Actually the village, and not the city, is the place for the development of the mind.

73. basala: a carpenter's tool

3.

World War II and After 1938–1946

Thus far we have seen Gandhi at the height of political action in India in the Salt March and then at the Second Round Table in London, and we have seen him back in India turning from political action toward hands-on work with people in villages and especially among the untouchables. At nearly 70, he has, in effect, retired from politics, and given his own preference, he would probably have spent the rest of his life on village uplift, promoting the spinning wheel, and working to ease the plight of the Harijans. But the larger world was changing. As early as 1931, Romain Rolland, writing to Gandhi, had used the phrase "Second World War." The phrase was prophetic.

In 1933, Adolph Hitler was appointed Chancellor of Germany. His rise to supreme power was rapid. By the end of the year, 92 percent of the German electorate supported Hitler, and Nazi parties had been organized in Czechoslovakia and Denmark. The following year Hitler met with Mussolini and formed the Axis, and in 1935 Mussolini attacked Abyssinia. In 1936 civil war broke out in Spain between Fascists and Loyalists. Partisans on both sides came from other countries to join the battle which ended with victory for the Fascists.

In China, Chiang Kai-Shek, the Nationalist leader, anticipating a Japanese attack, joined forces with Mao Tse Tung, the Communist leader, to defend China. The combined effort was not successful. Peking and other Chinese cities shortly fell to Japanese forces. Back in Europe, Hitler's forces took over Austria, and in 1938 moved on Czechoslovakia. British Prime Minister Chamberlain tried to "appease" Hitler, and was forced out of office. Germany mobilized its forces, and France called up reservists. The stage was set for World War II, which began on September 1, 1939 with Germany's invasion of Poland.

Gandhi in the meantime had been working with Abdul Ghaffar Khan, the Muslim leader of a nonviolent army in the frontier provinces of India.

Before and during the war, Gandhi and his colleagues had to deal with the issue of whether to work with the British or challenge them when they were tremendously preoccupied with the war and fearful of how India might influence the war. As one example of this, Subhas Chandra Bose led an effort to seek support from the Germans and the Japanese in order to take advantage of Britain's time of weakness.

During these years, Gandhi's roles changed rapidly. He was imprisoned for nearly two years. Harijan *was suspended by Gandhi himself for one period, and was suspended by the British for another period. So he was not always involved directly. And in the end, after the war was over, he again played a major if almost futile role in the struggles which ensued.*

Before the Outbreak of War

Kathryn Tidrick, in Gandhi: A Political and Spiritual Life, *writes that during the Salt March, "In the North-West the disturbances followed agitation by one of Gandhi's most surprising converts, Abdul Ghaffar Khan, whose Red Shirt movement brought Congress politics, Gandhian tactics and Pathan nationalism together in an unpredictable alliance" (234). Gandhi in 1938, when the war had not yet begun, took a page from Abdul Ghaffar Khan's non-violent actions in the Frontier Provinces, to propose the formation of peace brigades in India. Also known as Badshah Khan, Ghaffar Khan became known as "The Frontier Gandhi." A Muslim, brought up in an Afghan culture which depended on a violent response to violence, Badshah Khan rejected that approach and became a close ally to Gandhi. He lived to be 98 years old and spent thirty years in prisons, one third of his life, first under British and then Pakistani authorities (Eknath Easwaran,* Nonviolent Soldier of Islam: Badshah Khan, A Man to Match His Mountains, *186, 233).*

Qualifications of a Peace Brigade

June 18, 1938

Some time ago I suggested the formation of a Peace Brigade whose members would risk their lives in dealing with riots, especially communal.[74] The idea was that this Brigade should substitute for the police and even the military. This reads ambitious. The achievement may prove impossible. Yet, if the Congress is to succeed in its non-violent struggle, it must develop the power to deal peacefully with such situations. Communal riots are engineered by politically minded men. Many of those who take part in them are under the influence of the latter. Surely it should not be beyond the wit of Congressmen

74. communal: refers to violence involving different religious groups, e.g. Hindus and Muslims

to devise a method or methods of avoiding ugly communal situations by peaceful means. I say this irrespective of whether there is or there is not a communal pact. It cannot be that any party seeks to force a pact by violent means. Even if such a pact were a possibility, it would not be worth the paper on which it might be written. For behind such a pact there will be no common understanding. What is more, even after a pact is arrived at, it would be too much to expect that there would never be any communal riots.

Let us therefore see what qualifications a member of the contemplated Peace Brigade should possess.

1. He or she must have a living faith in non-violence. This is impossible without a living faith in God. A non-violent man can do nothing save by the power and grace of God. Without it he won't have the courage to die without anger, without fear and without retaliation. Such courage comes from the belief that God sits in the hearts of all and that there should be no fear in the presence of God. The knowledge of the omnipresence of God also means respect for the lives of even those who may be called opponents or goondas.[75] This contemplated intervention is a process of stilling the fury of man when the brute in him gets the mastery over him.

2. This messenger of peace must have equal regard for all the principal religions of the earth. If he is a Hindu, he will respect the other faiths current in India. He must therefore possess a knowledge of the different faiths professed in the country.

3. Generally speaking this work of peace can only be done by local men in their own localities.

4. The work can be done singly or in groups. Therefore no one need wait for companions. Nevertheless one would natu-

75. goondas: thugs

rally seek companions in one's own locality and form a local brigade.

5. This messenger of peace will cultivate through personal service contacts with the people in his locality or chosen circle, so that when he appears to deal with ugly situations, he does not descend upon the members of a riotous assembly as an utter stranger liable to be looked upon as a suspect or an unwelcome visitor.

6. Needless to say, a peace bringer must have a character beyond reproach and must be known for his strict impartiality.

7. Generally there are previous warnings of coming storms. If these are known, the peace brigade will not wait till the conflagration breaks out but will try to handle the situation in anticipation.

8. Whilst, if the movement spreads, it might be well if there are some whole-time workers, it is not absolutely necessary that there should be. The idea is to have as many good and true men and women as possible. These can be had only if volunteers are drawn from those who are engaged in various walks of life but have leisure enough to cultivate friendly relations with the people living in their circle and otherwise possess the qualifications required of a member of the Peace Brigade.

9. There should be a distinctive dress worn by the members of the contemplated brigade so that in course of time they will be recognized without the slightest difficulty.

These are but general suggestions. Each centre can work out its own constitution on the basis here suggested.

Lest false hopes may be raised, I must warn workers against entertaining the hope that I can play any active part in the formation of Peace Brigades. I have not the health, energy or time for it. I find it hard enough to cope with the tasks I dare not shirk. I can only guide and make suggestions through correspondence or these columns. Therefore let those who appreciate the idea and feel they have the ability, take the initiative themselves. I know that the proposed Brigade has great possibilities and that the idea behind it is quite capable of being worked out in practice.

These excerpts are drawn from an article written by Gandhi after the pre-World War II Munich agreement in which England and France yielded to Hitler's demands for the annexation of part of Czechoslovakia. Gandhi states an interesting position, which combines two crisis situations, one in Europe, the other in Afghanistan.

From: If I Were a Czech

October 6, 1938

... I want to speak to the Czechs because their plight moved me to the point of physical and mental distress and I felt it would be cowardice on my part not to share with them the thoughts that are welling up within me. It is clear that the small nations must either come or be ready to come under the protection of the dictators or be a constant menace to the peace of Europe. In spite of all the good will in the world England and France cannot save them. ... If I were a Czech, therefore, I would free these two nations from the obligation to defend my country. And yet I must live. I would not be a vassal to any nation or body. I must have absolute independence or perish. To seek to win in a clash of arms would be pure bravado. Not so, if in defying the might of one who would deprive me of my independence I refuse to obey his will and perish unarmed in the attempt. In so doing, though I lose the body, I save my soul, i.e., my honour. ...

This is how I should, I believe, act if I was a Czech. When I first launched out on Satyagraha, I had no companion. We were thirteen thousand men, women and children against a whole nation capable of crushing the existence out of us. I did not know who would listen to me. It all came as in a flash. All the 13,000 did not fight. Many fell back. But the honour of the nation was saved. New history was written by the South African Satyagraha.

A more apposite instance, perhaps, is that of Khansaheb Abdul Gaffar Khan, the servant of God as he calls himself, the pride of Afghan as the Pathans delight to call him. He is sitting in front of me as I pen these lines. He has made several thousand of his people throw down their arms. He thinks he has imbibed the lesson of non-violence. He is not sure of his people. … I have come to the Frontier Province, or rather he has brought me to see with my own eyes what his men here are doing. I can say in advance and at once that these men know very little of non-violence. All the treasure they have on earth is their leader. I do not cite these soldiers of peace as at all a finished illustration. I see them as an honest attempt by a soldier to convert fellow soldiers to the ways of peace. I can testify that it is an honest attempt, and whether in the end it succeeds or fails, it will have its lessons for satyagrahis of the future. My purpose will be fulfilled if I succeed in reaching these men's hearts and making them see that if their non-violence does not make them feel much braver than the possession of arms and the ability to use them they must give up their nonviolence, which is another name for cowardice, and resume their arms which there is nothing but their own will to prevent them from taking back.

I present Dr. Benes[76] with a weapon not of the weak but of the brave. There is no bravery greater than a resolute refusal to bend the knee to an earthly power, no matter how great, and that without bitterness of spirit and in the fullness of faith that the spirit alone lives, nothing else does.

Two days later Gandhi comes back to comment again on Czechoslovakia's dilemmas, providing a striking statement of nonviolence in desperate circumstances.

76. Edvard Benes (1884–1948), Foreign Minister and then President of Czechoslovakia, was "a founder of modern Czechoslovakia who forged its Western-oriented foreign policy between World Wars I and II but capitulated to Hitler's demands during the Czech crisis of 1938" (www.britannica.com).

Logical Consequence

October 8, 1938

One must feel happy that the danger of war has been averted for the time being. Is the price paid likely to be too great? Is it likely that honour has been restored? Is it a triumph of organized violence? Has Herr Hitler discovered a new technique of organizing violence which enables him to gain his end without shedding blood? I do not profess to known [sic] European politics. But it does appear to me that small nationalities cannot exist in Europe with their heads erect. They must be absorbed by their larger neighbours. They must become vassals.

Europe has sold her soul for the sake of a seven days' earthly existence. The peace Europe gained at Munich is a triumph of violence; it is also its defeat. If England and France were sure of victory, they would certainly have fulfilled their duty of saving Czechoslovakia or of dying with it. But they quailed before the combined violence of Germany and Italy. But what have Germany and Italy gained? Have they added anything to the moral wealth of mankind? ...

But the war is only postponed. During the breathing time, I present the way of non-violence for acceptance by the Czechs. They do not yet know what is in store for them. They can lose nothing by trying the way of non-violence. The fate of Republican Spain is hanging in the balance. So is that of China. If in the end they all lose, they will do so not because their cause is not just, but because they are less skilled in the science of destruction or because they are undermanned. What would Republican Spain gain if it had Franco's resources, or China if she had Japan's skill in war, or the Czechs if they had the skill of Herr Hitler? I suggest that if it is brave, as it is, to die to a man fighting against odds, it is braver still to refuse to fight and yet to refuse to yield to the usurper. If death is a certainty in either case, is it not nobler to die with the breast bared to the enemy without malice against him within?

Six weeks before the outbreak of World War II, on the advice of Western friends, Gandhi undertook to write a friendly letter to Hitler. From his Jewish friend Hermann Kallenbach, who was distraught and angry, Gandhi heard about the oppressive treatment the Jews were receiving. It seemed that *a letter to Hitler could do no harm, but the letter suggests a grievous misreading of Hitler's intentions. Robert Payne writes that Gandhi "addressed a strangely diffident and respectful letter to Hitler, which appears to have been written in a mood of profound hopelessness..." (485). Gandhi did not know that the Raj would not allow the letter to be sent (*CWMG-CD *76:156n3; Rajmohan Gandhi 421).*

Letter to Adolf Hitler

At Wardha, C. P. India
July 23, 1939

Dear Friend,

Friends have been urging me to write to you for the sake of humanity. But I have resisted their request, because of the feeling that any letter from me would be an impertinence. Something tells me that I must not calculate and that I must make my appeal for whatever it may be worth.

It is quite clear that you are today the one person in the world who can prevent a war which may reduce humanity to the savage state. Must you pay that price for an object however worthy it may appear to you to be? Will you listen to the appeal of one who has deliberately shunned the method of war not without considerable success? Anyway I anticipate your forgiveness, if I have erred in writing to you.

I remain,
Your sincere friend,

*Gandhi was struggling with what he saw happening. He thought a great deal about the oppression of the Jews and the growing violence. He wrote, "If there ever could be a justifiable war in the name of and for humanity, a war against Germany, to prevent the wanton persecution of a whole race, would be completely justified. But I do not believe in any war" (*Harijan *November 26, 1938). He believed that through satyagraha, and very possibly with huge numbers of casualties, the Jews could arouse the world and the people of Germany (Payne 486). Rajmohan Gandhi writes that his grandfather "did not know that in November 1937 Indian nonviolence and British appeasement of it were ridiculed by Hitler. Speaking to Irwin, now Lord Halifax* *and a minister under Chamberlain, Hitler had said, 'All you have to do is to shoot Gandhi. If necessary, shoot more leaders of Congress. You will be surprised how quickly the trouble will die down'" (400). Gandhi would write a second letter to Hitler on December 24, 1941, not realizing how such a letter would fall on deaf ears. That second letter was also suppressed by the government in India (*CWMG-CD *79:453n4).*

After the Outbreak of War

Almost immediately after the war had actually begun, Gandhi expresses on September 5, 1939, his sympathy for Britain and France and reveals the heartfelt searching and questioning he has gone through about the power of reason and the German people. By "His Excellency," Gandhi is referring to the Viceroy.

Statement to the Press

September 5, 1939

. . . I told His Excellency that my own sympathies were with England and France from the purely humanitarian standpoint. I told him that I could not contemplate without being stirred to the very depth the destruction of London which had hitherto been regarded as impregnable. And as I was picturing before him the Houses of Parliament and the Westminster Abbey and their possible destruction, I broke down. I have become disconsolate. In the secret of my heart I am in perpetual quarrel with God that He should allow such things to go on. My non-violence seems almost impotent. But the answer comes at the end of the daily quarrel that neither God nor non-violence is impotent. Impotence is in men. I must try on without losing faith even though I may break in the attempt. . . .

How I wish that even now he [Hitler] would listen to reason and the appeal from almost the whole of thinking mankind, not excluding the German people themselves. I must refuse to believe that Germans contemplate with equanimity the evacuation of big cities like London for fear of destruction to be wrought by man's inhuman ingenuity. They cannot contemplate with equanimity such destruction of themselves and their own monuments. I am not therefore just now thinking of India's deliverance. It will come, but what will it be worth if England and France fall, or if they come out victorious over Germany ruined and humbled?

Yet it almost seems as if Herr Hitler knows no God but brute force and, as Mr. Chamberlain says, he will listen to nothing else. It is in the midst of this catastrophe without parallel that Congressmen and all other responsible Indians individually and collectively have to decide what part India is to play in this terrible drama.

As the War goes on, Gandhi begins formulating questions about what the war will mean for India and other parts of the British Empire. Despite Prime Minister Chamberlain's denial of imperialism, Gandhi questions Britain's exploitation of other nations, while articulating India's independence and expressing trust finally in Britain to act morally.

Statement to "The New Chronicle"

Segaon
December 4, 1939

Mr. Chamberlain is reported to have said, "If imperialism means the assertion of racial superiority, suppression of political and economic freedom of other peoples, the exploitation of the resources of other countries, for the benefit of an imperialist country, then I say they are not the characteristics of this country." This is pleasing to the ear but does not square with the facts. The policy adopted in Kenya, the clove business in Zanzibar, the Ottawa Pact, not to speak of the Dominions which exploit the so-called uncivilized races of the earth do not show as if the imperial spirit was dead. ...

Also I fail to see why Britain's intention about India should be dependent upon Muslim, Hindu or any other opinion. The only opinion that counts is India's opinion, not even the Congress opinion. India's opinion can only be ascertained by the free vote of her people. ... So far as the Congress is concerned, the people of Princes' India should be represented precisely on the same footing as those of British India. The Muslims and other accepted minorities may be represented by separate electorates, if necessary, and in exact proportion to their numbers. They will determine what is required for their protection. In all matters of common interest a composite majority decision should prevail. If a better way than a Constituent Assembly can be found for knowing the will of the people, so far as I know, the Congress will accept it without hesitation. Neither the size of the country nor the illiteracy of the masses should be a bar against adult suffrage. The election campaign will itself be sufficient education for the purpose of broadly knowing the popular will.

The declaration of British policy about India is a purely moral issue, for freedom-loving India has neither the will nor the capacity to resort to armed revolt. Nevertheless, it is her right to know Britain's will about her. I am aware that Britain can impress men and money from India treated as her dependency, but she can get moral weight on her side only from an India conscious of her freedom. I am anxious, as a friend of Britain bound by many personal ties, that she should come out victorious not because of her superiority in the use of arms but because of her will to be just all along the line. She will then have the true friendship and sympathy of millions of people all over the world who have become sick of the wanton waste of precious life and of the palpable lies disseminated to sustain greed and hunger for dominion.

In February, Gandhi is ready to spell out a position with regard to India and the war. He addresses each of the major objections to granting Indian independence put forth by the British who argued, for example, that defense during the war made independence impossible. Gandhi's secretary, Mahadev Desai, describes Gandhi's meeting with the press: "On the morning of the 6th of February 1940 he ... received an army of journalists—representatives of the London papers ... and of the Associated Press of America. But for them he might have been sleeping the sleep of the just—after a ... momentous step which he has prayerfully taken. But he received them for an hour before taking the train for Wardha, and dictated to them a statement pausing only once to correct a word or a sentence" (CWMG-CD 77:300n1). The result is Gandhi's proposal for changed relations between Britain and India.

Statement to the Press

New Delhi
February 6, 1940

The vital difference between the Congress demand and the Viceregal offer consists in the fact that the Viceroy's offer contemplates the final determination of India's destiny by the British Government, whereas the Congress contemplates just the contrary. The Congress position is that the test of real freedom consists in the people of India determining their own destiny without any outside influence, and I see no prospect whatsoever of a peaceful and honourable settlement between England and India unless the vital difference is obliterated and England decides upon the right course, viz., accepts the position that the time has come when India must be allowed to determine her own constitution and her status. When that is done, the question of Defence, the question of minorities, the question of the Princes and the question of the European interest will automatically resolve itself.

Let me make this a little clearer. The provision of safeguards for the rights of minorities is not only common cause between the British Government and the Congress, but the Representative Assembly of Indians cannot evolve a stable Constitution without fullest satisfaction being given to the legitimate minorities. I use the word 'legitimate' advisedly because I see that minorities crop up like mushrooms, till there will be no majority left. By fullest satisfaction I mean satisfaction which will not militate against the progress of the nation as a whole. I will, therefore, in the event of differences, refer the question to the highest and most impartial tribunal that can be conceived by human ingenuity. Its voice shall be final as to what will amount to the fullest satisfaction of minority interests.

So far as Defence is concerned, surely it will be the primary concern of free India to make her own arrangements. It may well be that India would want elaborate preparation and would want Britain's help, if it is given, in enabling her to do so. Thanks to Imperial policy, unarmed India is left wholly unprotected except by the British bayonet and Indian soldiers whom British power has brought into being. It is a position humiliating alike for Britain and for India. I am personally unconcerned because, if I could carry India with me, I would want nothing beyond a police force for protection against dacoits[77] and the like. But so far as Defence is concerned unarmed peaceful India would rely upon the goodwill of the whole world. But I know that that is only a dream at the present moment.

So far as European interests are concerned, emphasis on the word 'European' must be entirely removed. But that does not mean that a free India should be free to confiscate European interests or any other interests. There would, as there should, be provision for reasonable compensation for any existing interests which are legitimate and not harmful to the nation. It follows that there can be no question of favouritism which is being enjoyed today by European interests, I would, therefore, regard them as big zamindars or capitalists. They will be put on the same footing as these.

So far as the Princes are concerned, they are free to join the national assembly which will determine India's fate not as individuals but as duly elected representatives of their own people. The Princes being vassals of the Crown, I fancy they have no status apart from the Crown, and certainly not superior to the Crown itself. And if the Crown parts with the power it enjoys over the whole of India, naturally the Princes have—and it should be their pride—to look up to the successor to the Crown, i.e., the people of India, for the preservation of their status.

I hope this will not be regarded as a tall claim, for it is made not on behalf of the Congress, nor of any single party, but on behalf of the unrepresented dumb millions of India. No claim made on their behalf can be considered too tall. I am myself an insignificant being, but I am supposed to have some hold over these dumb millions. I know that in every fibre of my being I am also one of them; and without them I am nothing and I do not even want to exist.

I want on their behalf an honourable settlement with Britain without even a non-violent fight. My dictionary has no such expression as a violent fight. Yesterday I put this view before His Excellency in as courteous and friendly a language as I was capable of using. We approached the discussion as personal friends, each believing in the other's sincerity. We understood each other, and both recognized that there still existed a wide gulf between the Government's position and the position taken by the Congress which I

77. dacoits: bandits

put, though not as an accredited representative of the Congress but certainly as the self-appointed representative of the dumb millions.

We parted as friends. I have no disappointment in me that the negotiations have failed. That failure I am going to use, as I am sure H. E. the Viceroy is going to use, as a stepping-stone to success. But if that success does not come in the near future, I can only say Heaven help India, Britain and the world. The present war must not be decided by a clash of arms, but it must be decided by the moral strength that each party can show. If Britain cannot recognize India's legitimate claim, what will it mean but Britain's moral bankruptcy?

[In answer to a question Gandhi went on to speak of the division between Congress and the Muslim League.]

I don't see any chance at present of approach between the Congress and the Muslim League.[78] I do not see any; because the Muslim League represented by Jinnah Saheb's letter to me takes up a position which is wholly inimical to the national cause. He contemplates several Indias. The Congress contemplates only one India. . . .

The next day, under the title, "Let Britain Abandon Her Immoral Hold," Gandhi amplified the previous statement. The two statements taken together give a fairly full picture of the situation as Gandhi saw it in the early stages of World War II, including his succinct view of the problems caused by imperialism. The war and the old arguments such as tensions among Indian factions were now insufficient reasons for refusing to grant independence. His bluntness reflects his resolve and determination.

78. The Muslim League was a political group, founded in 1906, which at first worked for Hindu-Muslim unity, but later called for a separate Muslim nation, leading to the partition of India and Pakistan (www.britannica.com).

Statement to *The Daily Herald*

Segaon
February 7, 1940

My interview with the Viceroy shows what wide gulf exists between British Government and nationalist India. What is offered is not real independence. Reality demands that India should determine what she needs, not Britain. There could be no justice or virtue in Britain yielding to successful rebellion, violent or non-violent. Will present problems be then deemed to be dissolved? It is necessary for Britain to be just to declare her determination to recognize immediately the freedom of India in practice, and the constitution to be framed by the Constituent Assembly or an equivalent as soon as practicable. There is no analogy between the Dominions and India. Hers is a case by itself and has to be treated as such. It should be clearly understood that every problem is of Britain's own making. What has happened was no doubt a necessity of imperialism. But if imperialism dies, the problems of Britain's making will be automatically dissolved. Defense is the greatest of all. Why did Britain disarm India? Why have even Indian soldiers become foreigners in their own land? Why did Britain create Princes and arm them with unheard-of powers? Surely for making her foothold secure. Who created the gigantic European interests, and why? Who created minorities? There is no majority save the political majority. But these four were and still are bulwarks of imperialism. No jugglery of words can hide this naked truth. Britain's moral victory will be assured when she decides by a mighty effort to abandon her immoral hold on India; and then her other victory will follow as day follows night. For then, the conscience of the whole world will be on her side. No makeshift such as is now offered can stir India's heart or world conscience.

In April Gandhi found it necessary to state his position with regard to the Muslim desire for a separate state, a struggle which would eventually end in the division of India, with great violence and bloodshed. He cannot "forcibly resist" partition but he can bring to bear the strongest arguments possible. The location from which he issues this statement is Sevagram, the name now given to the ashram at Segaon.

My Position

Sevagram
April 9, 1940

... As a man of non-violence I cannot forcibly resist the proposed partition if the Muslims of India really insist upon it. But I can never be a willing party to the vivisection. I would employ every non-violent means to prevent it. For it means the undoing of centuries of work done by numberless Hindus and Muslims to live together as one nation. Partition means a patent untruth. My whole soul rebels against the idea that Hinduism and Islam represent two antagonistic cultures and doctrines. To assent to such a doctrine is for me denial of God. For I believe with my whole soul that the God of the Quran is also the God of the Gita, and that we are all, no matter by what name designated, children of the same God. I must rebel against the idea that millions of Indians who were Hindus the other day changed their nationality on adopting Islam as their religion.

But that is my belief. I cannot thrust it down the throats of the Muslims who think that they are a different nation. I refuse, however, to believe that the eight crores[79] of Muslims will say that they have nothing in common with their Hindu and other brethren. Their mind can only be known by a referendum duly made to them on that clear issue. The contemplated Constituent Assembly can easily decide the question. Naturally on an issue such as this there can be no arbitration. It is purely and simply a matter of self-determination. I know of no other conclusive method of ascertaining the minds of the eight crores of Muslims. ...

By June 1940 Hitler's armies had gone around the so-called Maginot line and invaded France. Paris had fallen, and the French had surrendered. In this article Gandhi draws upon his experience in South Africa to apply the principles of nonviolence to this changed situation in Europe. Falling between his two letters addressed directly to Hitler, this statement shows Gandhi as less naive about Hitler than the letters suggest. Gandhi's analogy, which takes the long view of generations, refers to those who would resist Hitler with military might.

79. crore: 10 million

How to Combat Hitlerism

Sevagram
June 18, 1940

Whatever Hitler may ultimately prove to be, we know what Hitlerism has come to mean. It means naked ruthless force reduced to an exact science and worked with scientific precision. In its effect it becomes almost irresistible.

In the early days of satyagraha when it was still known as passive resistance, The Star of Johannesburg, stirred by the sight of a handful of Indians, wholly unarmed and incapable of organised violence even if they wished it, pitting themselves against an overwhelmingly armed Government, had a cartoon in which the latter was depicted as a steam-roller representing irresistible force, and passive resistance was depicted as an elephant unmoved and comfortably planting himself in his seat. This was marked immovable force. The cartoonist had a true insight into the duel between the irresistible and the immovable forces. It was then a stalemate. The sequel we know. What was depicted and appeared to be irresistible was successfully resisted by the immovable force of satyagraha—call it suffering without retaliation.

What became true then can be equally true now. Hitlerism will never be defeated by counter-Hitlerism. It can only breed superior Hitlerism raised to nth degree. What is going on before our eyes is a demonstration of the futility of violence as also of Hitlerism.

Let me explain what I mean by failure of Hitlerism. It has robbed the small nations of their liberty. It has compelled France to sue for peace. Probably by the time this is in print Britain will have decided upon her course. The fall of France is enough for my argument. I think French statesmen have shown rare courage in bowing to the inevitable and refusing to be party to senseless mutual slaughter. There can be no sense in France coming out victorious if the stake is in truth lost. The cause of liberty becomes a mockery if the price to be paid is wholesale destruction of those who are to enjoy liberty. It then becomes an inglorious satiation of ambition. The bravery of the French soldier is world-known. But let the world know also the greater bravery of the French statesmen in suing for peace. I have assumed that the French statesmen have taken the step in a perfectly honourable manner as behooves true soldiers. Let me hope that Herr Hitler will impose no humiliating terms but show that, though he can fight without mercy, he can at least conclude peace not without mercy.

But to resume the thread of the argument, What will Hitler do with his victory? Can he digest so much power? Personally he will go as empty-handed as his not very remote predecessor Alexander. For the Germans he will have left not the pleasure of owning a mighty empire but the burden of sustaining its crushing weight. For they will not be able to hold all the conquered nations in perpetual subjection. And I doubt if the Germans of future generations will entertain unadulterated pride in the deeds for which Hitlerism will be deemed responsible. They will honour Herr Hitler as a genius, as a brave man, a matchless organizer and much more. But I should hope that the Germans of the future will have learnt the art of discrimination even about their heroes. Anyway I think it will be allowed that all the blood that has been spilled by Hitler has added not a millionth part of an inch to the world's moral stature.

As against this imagine the state of Europe today if the Czechs, the Poles, the Norwegians, the French and the English had all said to Hitler: "You need not make your scientific preparation for destruction. We will meet your violence with non-violence. You will therefore be able to destroy our non-violent army without tanks, battleships and airships." It may be retorted that the only difference would be that Hitler would have got without fighting what he has gained after a bloody fight. Exactly. The history of Europe would then have been written differently. Possession might (but only might) have been then taken under non-violent resistance, as it has been taken now after perpetration of untold barbarities. Under non-violence only those would have been killed who had trained themselves to be killed, if need be, but without killing anyone and without bearing malice towards anybody. I dare say that in that case Europe would have added several inches to its moral stature. And in the end I expect it is the moral worth that will count. All else is dross.

I have written these lines for the European Powers. But they are meant for ourselves. If my argument has gone home, is it not time for us to declare our changeless faith in non-violence of the strong and say we do not seek to defend our liberty with the force of arms but we will defend it with the force of non-violence?

Two months later, writing in Harijan, Gandhi goes back to the idea of a police force. He acknowledges that police will need arms for dealing with criminals, but he would change their relationship with the community regarding all other disputes.

My Idea of a Police Force

Sevagram
August 20, 1940

A friend writes as follows:

> ... Can we envisage an order of society in which we will not have to resort to himsa[80] in any form whatsoever? Suppose for argument's sake that there exists a society where the majority does not possess goods that would excite envy and where everyone has the wherewithal to live contentedly. Even then it does not seem possible that there will be no disputes over proprietorship of land, lending and borrowing of money, and other business dealings. For these, therefore, we must provide the means of justice and see that the decisions of the courts or arbitration boards are carried out. For this it will be essential to have a police force. You have yielded this point. But I should like to know what restrictions you would place on the police force. If there were a non-violent Government in power today, would it use the police force for quelling internal disorders? And are you willing to maintain it for all time or only temporarily? My mind refuses to go so far as to envisage a time when a police force will be a superfluity. There seems to be no escape from placing this limitation, as it were, on ahimsa.[81]

80. himsa: violence or envy

81. ahimsa: nonviolence, non-injury, non-destruction of life

The questions asked in this letter are of the utmost importance and deserve notice. If true ahimsa had come into being within us, and if our so-called satyagraha movements had been truly non-violent, these questions would not have arisen because they would have been solved.

For one who has never seen the arctic regions an imaginary description of them, however elaborate, can convey but an inadequate idea of the reality. Even so is it with ahimsa. If all Congressmen had been true to their creed, we would not be vacillating between violence and non-violence as we are to-day. The fruits of ahimsa would be in evidence everywhere. There would be communal harmony, the demon of untouchability would have been cast out, and, generally speaking, we would have evolved an ordered society. But the reverse is the case just now. There is even definite hostility to the Congress in certain quarters. The word of Congressmen is not always relied on. The Muslim League and most of the Princes have no faith in the Congress and are in fact inimical to it. If Congressmen had true ahimsa in them, there would be none of this distrust. In fact the Congress would be the beloved of all.

Therefore I can only place an imaginary picture before the votaries of ahimsa.

So long as we are not saturated with pure ahimsa we cannot possibly win Swaraj through non-violence. We can come into power only when we are in a majority or, in other words, when the large majority of people are willing to abide by the law of ahimsa. When this happy state prevails the spirit of violence will have all but vanished and internal disorder will have come under control.

Nevertheless I have conceded that even in a non-violent State a police force may be necessary....

The police of my conception will, however, be of a wholly different pattern from the present-day force. Its ranks will be composed of believers in non-violence. They will be servants, not masters, of the people. The people will instinctively render them every help, and through mutual co-operation they will easily deal with the ever-decreasing disturbances. The police force will have some kind of arms, but they will be rarely used, if at all. In fact the policemen will be reformers. Their police work will be confined primarily to robbers and dacoits. Quarrels between labour and capital and strikes will be few and far between in a non-violent State, because the influence of the non-violent majority will be so great as to command the respect of the principal elements in society. Similarly there will be no room for communal disturbances. Then we must remember that when such a Congress Government comes into power the large majority of men and women of 21 years and over will have been enfranchised. The rigid and cramped constitution of today has of course no place in this picture.

In the same issue of Harijan, *writing while the Nazis were solidifying their control of western Europe, Gandhi turned his attention to economics. At this point, as with other matters, he was concerned with what people can do on a more or less individual basis, calling on the wealthy to make a voluntary, radical shift in their uses of their wealth. His belief here rests in faith in what can be accomplished without force, not in the Soviet communist meaning of "redistribution of wealth."*

Equal Distribution

Sevagram
August 19, 1940

... The real implication of equal distribution is that each man shall have the wherewithal to supply his natural needs and no more. For example, if one man has a weak digestion and requires only a quarter of a pound of flour for his bread and another needs a pound, both should be in a position to satisfy their wants. To bring this ideal into being the entire social order has got to be reconstructed. A society based on non-violence cannot nurture any other ideal. ...

It is perfectly possible for an individual to adopt this way of life without having to wait for others to do so. And if an individual can observe a certain rule of conduct, it follows that a group of individuals can do likewise ... no one need wait for anyone else in order to adopt a right course. Men generally hesitate to make a beginning if they feel that the objective cannot be had in its entirety. Such an attitude of mind is in reality a bar to progress.

Now let us consider how equal distribution can be brought about through non-violence. The first step towards it is for him who has made this ideal part of his being to bring about the necessary changes in his personal life. He would reduce his wants to a minimum, bearing in mind the poverty of India. His earnings would be free of dishonesty. The desire for speculation would be renounced. His habitation would be in keeping with the new mode of life. There would be self-restraint exercised in every sphere of life. When he has done all that is possible in his own life, then only will he be in a position to preach this ideal among his associates and neighbours.

Indeed at the root of this doctrine of equal distribution must lie that of the trusteeship of the wealthy for the superfluous wealth possessed by them. For according to the doctrine they may not possess a rupee more than their neighbours. How is this to be brought about? Non-violently? Or should the wealthy be dispossessed of their possessions? To do this we would naturally have to resort to violence. This violent action cannot benefit society. Society will be the poorer, for it will lose the gifts of a man who knows how to accumulate wealth. Therefore the non-violent way is evidently superior. The rich man will be left in possession of his wealth, of which he will use what he reasonably requires for his personal needs and will act as a trustee for the remainder to be used for the society. In this argument honesty on the part of the trustee is assumed.

As soon as a man looks upon himself as a servant of society, earns for its sake, spends for its benefit, then purity enters into his earnings and there is ahimsa in his venture. Moreover, if men's minds turn towards this way of life, there will come about a peaceful revolution in society, and that without any bitterness.

It may be asked whether history at any time records such a change in human nature. Such changes have certainly taken place in individuals. One may not perhaps be able to point to them in a whole society. But this only means that up till now there has never been an experiment on a large scale in non-violence. Somehow or other the wrong belief has taken possession of us that ahimsa is pre-eminently a weapon for individuals and its use should therefore be limited to that sphere. In fact this is not the case. Ahimsa is definitely an attribute of society. To convince people of this truth is at once my effort and my experiment. In this age of wonders no one will say that a thing or idea is worthless because it is new. To say it is impossible because it is difficult is again not in consonance with the spirit of the age. Things undreamt of are daily being seen, the impossible is ever becoming possible. We are constantly being astonished these days at the amazing discoveries in the field of violence. But I maintain that far more undreamt of and seemingly impossible discoveries will be made in the field of non-violence. The history of religion is full of such examples. To try to root out religion itself from society is a wild goose chase. And were such an attempt to succeed it would mean the destruction of society. … The ultimate definition of religion may be said to be obedience to the law of God. God and His law are synonymous terms. Therefore God signifies an unchanging and living law. No one has ever really found Him. But avatars and prophets have by means of their 'tapasya,'[82] given to mankind a faint glimpse of the eternal law.

If, however, in spite of the utmost effort, the rich do not become guardians of the poor in the true sense of the term and the latter are more and more crushed and die of hunger, what is to be done? In trying to find the solution to this riddle, I have lighted on non-violent non-cooperation and civil disobedience as the right and infallible means. The rich cannot accumulate wealth without the co-operation of the poor in society. Man has been conversant with violence from the beginning, for he has inherited this strength from the animal in his nature. It was only when he rose from the state of a quadruped (animal) to that of a biped (man) that the knowledge of the strength of ahimsa entered into his soul. This knowledge has grown within him slowly but surely. If this knowledge were to penetrate and spread amongst the poor, they would become strong and would learn how to free themselves by means of non-violence from the crushing inequalities which have brought them to the verge of starvation.

I scarcely need to write anything about non-cooperation and civil disobedience, for the readers of *Harijanbandu* are familiar with these and their working.

In September 1940, however, the position of India in the struggle had become a matter for political action. Gandhi had talks with the current Viceroy, Lord Linlithgow, about freedom of speech in war-time. The excerpts below are from two letters between the Viceroy and Gandhi.

82. tapasya: self-discipline, religious penance; sacrifice; austerity

From Viceroy-Gandhi Correspondence

September 30, 1940

Dear Mr. Gandhi,

... As you will remember, you wrote to me on the 18th September to ask that I should grant you an interview, and you explained in your letter that you were anxious to discuss the situation covered by the recent resolution of the All India Congress Committee, not only in your capacity as guide of the Congress but as a personal friend. I was, I need not say, most ready to talk things over with you, and we have now had the advantage of two conversations.

In the course of these conversations the situation has been exhaustively discussed, with particular reference to the question of free speech in time of war. On that matter, while professing yourself most anxious to avoid in any way embarrassing His Majesty's Government in the prosecution of the war, you made it clear to me that you regarded it as essential that the Indian National Congress and other members of the public should be in a position to give full expression to their views in relation to the war effort, provided only that such expression was fully non-violent.

I indicated to you the nature of the special treatment laid down by law in the United Kingdom for dealing with conscientious objectors—which I may broadly describe as an arrangement under which, while the conscientious objector is absolved from the duty of fighting and is allowed even to profess his faith in public, he is not permitted to carry his opposition to the length of endeavouring to persuade others, whether soldiers or munitions workers, to abandon their allegiance or to discontinue their effort.

You made it clear to me that you would not regard treatment of that nature as adequate in the conditions of India, and that you regarded it as essential that in India, where in your judgment conditions were wholly different from those existing in Great Britain, the Indian objector, either to all war as such, or to the participation of India in the present war, should be untrammeled in the expression of his views.

It emerged further from our conversation that, while you would not yourself preach to workers engaged in war work at the actual works, in an endeavour there to dissuade them from working on war equipment, you would regard it as essential that it should be open to Congressmen and non-Congressmen alike to deliver addresses and otherwise to call upon people throughout the country to refrain from assisting India's war effort in any way which would involve India's participation in bloodshed.

I listened with the utmost care and attention to your argument, and our examination of the situation has been full and close. I felt bound, however, in the outcome to make it clear to you that action such as you suggest would certainly amount not only to the inhibition of India's war effort, but to that embarrassment of Great Britain in the prosecution of the war which the Congress state that they are anxious to avoid; and that it would clearly not be possible in the interests of India herself, more particularly at this most critical juncture in the war, to acquiesce in the interference with the war effort which would be involved in freedom of speech so wide as that for which you had asked.

Gandhiji's Reply

September 30, 1940

Dear Lord Linlithgow:

I have your letter of even date. It fairly sets forth the Congress position as I placed it before you. It is a matter of deep regret to me that the Government have not been able to appreciate the Congress position, meant just to satisfy the bare requirements of the people, whether Congressmen or others, who felt a conscientious objection to helping a war to which they were never invited and which they regard, so far as they are concerned, as one for saving Imperialism, of which India is the greatest victim. Their objection is just as conscientious as mine as a war resister. I cannot claim greater freedom for my conscience than for that of those I have named.

As I made it plain in the course of our talks, the Congress is as much opposed to victory for Nazism as any Britisher can be. But their objection cannot be carried to the extent of their participation in the war. And since you and the Secretary of State for India have declared that the whole of India is voluntarily helping the war effort, it becomes necessary to make clear that the vast majority of the people of India are not interested in it. They make no distinction between Nazism and the double autocracy that rules India. Had

His Majesty's Government recognized the freedom required in the special condition of India, they would have justified the claim that they were receiving from India only such effort as they could voluntarily. The war party and the no-war party would have been placed on an equal footing so far as each worked fully non-violently.

As to the last paragraph of your letter, I wish to remind you that it was never contemplated to carry non-embarrassment to the point of self-extinction or, in other words, stopping all national activities which are designed to make India peace-minded and show that India's participation could not benefit anyone, not excluding Great Britain. Indeed I hold that, if India were left free to make her choice which freedom of speech implied, India would probably have turned the scales in favour of Britain and true liberty by the moral prestige which Britain would have then gained.

I must, therefore, repeat that the Congress does still want to refrain from embarrassing the British Government in their war effort. But it is impossible for the Congress to make of the policy a fetish by denying its creed at this critical period in the history of mankind. If the Congress has to die, it should do so in the act of proclaiming its faith. It is unfortunate that we have not been able to arrive at an agreement on the single issue of freedom of speech. But I shall hug the hope that it will be possible for the Government to work out their policy in the spirit of the Congress position.

I should like to touch upon the other points I raised in our talks. But for fear of burdening this reply, I refrain. I shall hope to make a public statement on them as early as I can.

In conclusion, let me thank you publicly for the great courtesy and patience with which you listened to my very long statement and argument. And though our ways seem to diverge for the moment, our personal friendship will, as you have kindly said at the time of saying farewell, bear the strain of divergence.

As arranged I am handing our correspondence to the Press for publication.

Gandhi's approach to civil disobedience in the face of war is a kind of culmination of many of his principal concerns. He proposes civil disobedience by one person, Vinoba Bhave[83]*—whom he will later designate as his successor. He has chosen a man who is committed to all of his own major concerns, the constructive program, the abolition of untouchability, the conflict between Hindus and Muslims. In the following, Gandhi asks his followers to refrain from violence. In doing all this he is demonstrating that a single individual may be able to make radical changes in the world, and in several matters at the same time.*

Civil Disobedience

Sevagram

October 15, 1940

I have had three days' discussion with the Working Committee. During it I unfolded my plan of civil disobedience in so far as I was able to envisage it. Although I have full charge of the campaign I could not think of taking the first step without consultation with the members of the Working Committee. In non-violent action one has to carry the co-workers with one through the mind and the heart. There is no other way to enforce discipline or obedience to instructions....

The plan is simply this. Direct action will be commenced by Shri Vinoba Bhave and for the time being confined to him only. And since it is to be confined to individual civil disobedience and that too of him only, it will be so conducted by him as to exclude others directly or indirectly. But since it is concerned with freedom of speech the public will be involved to an extent. It is open to them either to listen to him or not.

But much will depend upon what the Government wish to do. In spite of all attempts to confine civil disobedience to individuals and for the moment

83. Vinoba Bhave (1895–1982), as a young man in 1916, was on his way to Kashi (Varanasi, the Hindu holy city on the banks of Ganges River) to study Sanskrit when he stopped at Gandhi's ashram. Bhave was so moved by his first encounters with Gandhi that he almost immediately joined the ashram and postponed his studies. After Gandhi's death, he became most well known for his "Gift of Land" program; he walked over much of India gathering gifts of thousands of acres from landowners and then redistributed the land to the poor. He was chosen for the cover of *Time* magazine May 11, 1953 (www.mkgandhi-sarvodaya.org; www.culturalindia.net).

to one only, they can precipitate a crisis by making it a crime to listen to him or read anything written by him. But I think and believe that they do not want to invite any trouble, though they hold themselves in readiness to cope with every trouble that may face them....

Who is Vinoba Bhave and why has he been selected? He is an undergraduate having left college after my return to India in 1916. He is a Sanskrit scholar. He joined the Ashram almost at its inception. He was among the first members. In order to better qualify himself he took one year's leave to prosecute further studies in Sanskrit. And practically at the same hour at which he had left the Ashram a year before, he walked into it without notice... He has taken part in every menial activity of the Ashram from scavenging to cooking. Though he has a marvellous memory and is a student by nature, he has devoted the largest part of his time to spinning in which he has specialised as very few have. He believes in universal spinning being the central activity which will remove the poverty in the villages and put life into their deadness....

He has abolished every trace of untouchability from his heart. He believes in communal unity with the same passion that I have. In order to know the best mind of Islam he gave one year to the study of the Quran in the original. He therefore learnt Arabic. He found this study necessary for cultivating a living contact with the Muslims living in his neighbourhood....

Vinoba is an out and out war resister. But he respects equally with his own the conscience of those who, while not being out and out war resisters, have yet strong conscientious objection to participation in the present war. Though Vinoba represents both the types I may want to select another who will represent only one type, namely conscientious objection to participation in the present war.

It was necessary to introduce Vinoba at length to the public in order to justify my choice. This will perhaps be the last civil disobedience struggle which I shall have conducted. Naturally I would want it to be as flawless as it can be. Moreover the Congress has declared that it will avoid all avoidable embarrassment to the Government consistently with its own existence....

But Vinoba must fail, as I must, if we do not represent the Congress, let alone the whole nation. And we shall certainly not represent either if they do not give us full-hearted co-operation which is ceaseless prosecution of the constructive programme. It is not vocal co-operation that is required. It is co-operation in work that is needed. The signs of such co-operation will be phenomenal progress in spinning, complete disappearance of untouchability, and increasing friendliness between communities, and an increasing sense of justice in every walk of life. Unless rock bottom justice and equality pervade society surely there is no non-violent atmosphere. Above all, there should be no civil disobedience but what is sanctioned by me. This is peremptory obligation binding on every Congressman. If it is disregarded, there is no co-operation. The representative character belonging to Vinoba and me is then challenged. And I can say with confidence that, if the full-hearted co-operation I want is forthcoming, not only will the issue of freedom of speech be decided in our favour but we shall have gone very near Independence. …

Let me repeat the issue. On the surface it is incredibly narrow—the right to preach against war as war or participation in the present war. Both are matters of conscience for those who hold either view. Both are substantial rights. Their exercise can do no harm to the British if their pretension that to all intents and purposes India is an independent country is at all true. If India is very much a dependency in fact as it is in law, whatever the British get from India can never be regarded as voluntary, it must be regarded as impressed. This battle of life and death cannot be won by impressed levies, however large. They may win if they have the moral backing of an India truly regarded as free. Non-violent Congress cannot wish ill to Britain. Nor can it help her through arms since it seeks to gain her own freedom not through arms but through unadulterated non-violence. And the Congress vanishes if, at the crucial moment, it suppresses itself for fear of consequences or otherwise by ceasing to preach non-violence through non-violent means. So when we probe the issue deep enough we discover that it is a matter of life and death for us. If we vindicate that right, all is well with us. If we do not, all is lost. We cannot then win Swaraj through non-violent means.

I know that India has not one mind. There is a part of India that is war-minded and will learn the art of war through helping the British. The Congress has no desire, therefore, to surround ammunition factories or barracks and prevent people from doing what they like. We want to tell the people of India that, if they will win Swaraj through non-violent means, they may not co-operate militarily with Britain in the prosecution of the war.

This right of preaching against participation in war is being denied us, and we have to fight against the denial. Therefore while that right will be exercised only by those whom I may select for the purpose, all the other activities of the Congress will continue as before unless the Government interfere with them.

A question has been asked why, if I attach so much importance to quality, I do not offer civil resistance myself. I have already said that unlike as on previous occasions I do not wish to do so for the very good reason that my imprisonment is likely to cause greater embarrassment to the authorities than anything else the Congress can do. I want also to remain outside to cope with any contingency that may arise. My going to jail may be interpreted as a general invitation to all Congressmen to follow suit. They will not easily distinguish between my act and speech. Lastly, I do not know how things will shape. I myself do not know the next step. I do not know the Government plan. I am a man of faith. My reliance is solely on God. One step is enough for me. The next He will make clear to me when the time for it comes. And who knows that I shall not be an instrument for bringing about peace not only between Britain and India but also between the warring nations of the Earth. This last will not be taken for vanity for those who believe that my faith is not a sham but a reality greater than the fact that I am penning these lines.

At this point, the British authorities responded by ordering the suspension of the publication of Harijan. *Gandhi issued the following statement to the press.*

Why Suspension

October 24, 1940

On the 18th instant the Editor of *Harijan* received the following notice from the District Magistrate's office, Poona:

> I am directed by Government to advise you that no account of incidents leading up to satyagraha by Vinoba Bhave and no report of his speeches or any subsequent developments should be published without previous reference to the Chief Press Advisor, Delhi.

> I would like to bring to your notice that this is in your own interest to avoid prosecution under Rule 38 of the Defence of India Rules.

Thereupon I entered into correspondence with H. E. the Viceroy. Correspondence is still going on. But it is necessary for me to take a decision today for, if I did not, there may be waste of public money. In view of the reply hitherto received I have no course left open but to suspend publication of *Harijan*, *Harijanbandhu*, and *Harijansevak*. I cannot function freely if I have to send to the Press Advisor at New Delhi every line I write about satyagraha. It is true that the notice is only advisory, and that therefore I am not bound to act up to it. But the consequence of disregard of advice is also stated in the notice. I have no desire to risk a prosecution against the Editors. The three weeklies have been conducted in the interest of truth and therefore of all parties concerned. But I cannot serve that interest if the editing has to be done under threat of prosecution. Liberty of the Press is a dear privilege, apart from the advisability or otherwise of civil disobedience. The Government have shown their intention by the prosecution of Shri Vinoba Bhave. I have no complaint to make against the prosecution. It was an inevitable result of the Defence of India Rules. But the liberty of the Press stands on a different footing. I am unable to reconcile myself to the notice which, although in the nature of advice, is in reality an order whose infringement will carry its own consequences....

Expansion of the War

With that statement the publication was discontinued. A little over a year later, the entry of Japan into the war changed the strategic position of India. What had been mostly a European war had now become a World War. Japanese forces were invading Burma. Political leaders in India took various positions. Some saw this invasion as a threat to India; others, such as Subhas Chandra Bose and his followers, argued for making common cause with the Japanese and using this opportunity to throw off the British yoke. Gandhi, in what follows, maintains his non-violent position.

Discussion at Working Committee Meeting

[On or before December 30, 1941]

So far as I am concerned, even if I was given the utmost power conceivable, even if I was made the Viceroy of India today, would I ask the people of India to take up the sword to keep the Empire alive? I for one should feel that I was committing moral suicide in that I would be abandoning the faith of a lifetime, the faith which I had persuaded the Congress to accept for twenty years as a policy. The steady unflinching pursuit of that policy has brought us quite close to the achievement of the objective. Am I to abandon the very boat which has brought me quite close to the shore? Yudhishthira[84] would not forsake his faithful dog and enter the gates of heaven without him. For he knew that the Kingdom of Heaven would be as naught to him without the dog. i.e., his faith. Would the Arab (i.e., the Congress) give up towards the end of the journey the faithful steed (i.e., non-violence) that had made it possible for [him] to make that journey? It would be an act of betrayal or faithlessness on my part. Could I, when the war is at my door and when I am in the same predicament as they, forget the sovereign remedy I suggested to them and clutch at the method I have denounced and discarded? No matter what the country would say, what should be the attitude of individual Congressmen who had sworn by the method of non-violence?

At the same time, Gandhi was pursuing the idea of a Hindu universalism, which honored one's own faith as well as others, avoided denigrating other religions, and let each be what it is in relation to others. Here he replies to a Hindu who accuses him of betraying their religion.

84. Yudhishthira: one of the five brothers in the Mahabharata, one of the major Sanskrit religious epics in ancient India, along with the Ramayana

The Ashram Prayer

Sevagram
February 2, 1942

The Ashram prayer has become very popular. Its development has been spontaneous. The Ashram Bhajanavali (Hymn Book) has gone into several editions and is increasingly in demand. The birth and growth of this prayer has not been artificial. There is a history attached to almost every shloka[85] and every selected bhajan. The Bhajanavali contains among others bhajans from Muslim Sufis and Fakirs, from Guru Nanak, and from the Christian Hymnary. Every religion seems to have found a natural setting in the prayer book.

Chinese, Burmese, Jews, Ceylonese, Muslims, Parsis, Europeans and Americans have all lived in the Ashram from time to time. In the same way two Japanese sadhus[86] came to me in Maganwadi in 1935. One of them was with me till the other day when war broke out with Japan. He was an ideal inmate of our home in Sevagram. He took part in every activity with zest. I never heard of his quarrelling with anyone. He was a silent worker. He learnt as much Hindi as he could. He was a strict observer of his vows. Every morning and evening he could be seen going round with his drum and heard chanting his mantra.[87] The evening worship always commenced with his mantra.... "I bow to the Buddha, the giver of true religion." I shall never forget the quickness, the orderliness, and utter detachment with which he prepared himself the day the police came without notice to take him away from the Ashram. He took leave of me after reciting his favourite mantra and left his drum with me. "You are leaving us, but your mantra will remain an integral part of our Ashram prayer," were the words that came spontaneously to my lips. Since then, in spite of his absence, our morning and evening worship has commenced with the mantra. For me it is a constant reminder of Sadhu Keshav's purity and single-eyed devotion. Indeed its efficacy lies in that sacred memory.

---

85. shloka: prayer, song, stanza

86. sadhus: holy men

87. mantra: sound or word used to focus meditation

While Sadhu Keshav was still with us Bibi Raihana Tyabji came also to stay at Sevagram for a few days. I knew her to be a devout Muslim but was not aware, before the death of her illustrious father, of how well-versed she was in Koran Sharif.[88] When that jewel of Gujarat, Tyabji Saheb, expired no sound of weeping broke the awful silence in his room. The latter echoed with Bibi Raihana's sonorous recitation of verses from the Koran. Such as Abbas Tyabji Saheb cannot die. He is ever alive in the example of national service which he has left behind. Bibi Raihana is an accomplished singer with an ample repertory of bhajans of all kinds. She used to sing daily as well as recite beautiful verses from the Koran. I asked her to teach some verses to any of the inmates who could learn them, and she gladly did so. Like so many who come here she had become one of us. Raihana went away when her visit was over, but she has left a fragrant reminder of herself. The well-known 'al Fateha' has been included in the Ashram worship. The following is a translation of it:

1. I take refuge in Allah from Satan the accursed.

2. Say: He is God, the one and only
God, the Eternal, Absolute,
He begetteth not nor is He begotten,
And there is none like unto Him.

3. Praise be to God,
The Cherisher and Sustainer of the worlds,
Most Gracious, most Merciful,
Master of the Day of Judgment,
Thee do we worship
And Thine aid do we seek.
Show us the straight way.
The way of those on whom
Thou hast bestowed Thy Grace,
Those whose (portion) is not wrath
And who go not astray.

88. Koran Sharif: the holy Koran (Quran)

I am writing this note in reply to an ardent Hindu friend who has thus gently reproached me: "You have now given the Kalma[89] a place in the Ashram. What further remains to be done to kill your Hinduism?"

I am confident that my Hinduism and that of the other Ashram Hindus has grown thereby. There should be in us an equal reverence for all religions. Badshah Khan, whenever he comes, joins in the worship here with delight. He loves the tune to which the Ramayana is sung, and he listens intently to the Gita. His faith in Islam has not lessened thereby. Then why may I not listen to the Koran with equal reverence and adoration in my heart?

Vinoba and Pyrelal[90] studied Arabic and learnt the Koran in jail. Their Hinduism has been enriched by this study. I believe that Hindu-Muslim unity will come only through such spontaneous mingling of hearts and no other. Rama is not known by only a thousand names. His names are innumerable and He is the same whether we call him Allah, Khuda, Rahim, Razzak, the Bread giver, or any name that comes from the heart of a true devotee.

Meanwhile, Gandhi sees the need to reassure those who are worried about what is happening in the war. The two articles that follow are intended to assuage the fears of Japanese attacks on India.

Plea for Calmness

On the Train to Calcutta
February 17, 1942

The recent British reverses ought not to create panic in the land. In all the wars that Britain has fought or in which she has been engaged there have been reverses some which may be considered disastrous. But the British have

89. Kalma: Islamic prayer beginning "there is no God but Allah"

90. Pyarelal (Pyrelal) Nayar (1900–1982) belonged to Gandhi's closest group of aides, which included Mahadev Desai, Maganlal Gandhi (a nephew), Mirabehn, and Gandhi's son Devadas (Rajmohan Gandhi 283). These are the people who spent the most time with him. Pyarelal became Gandhi's personal secretary, later in life, and particularly after Mahadev Desai's death. (See Sushila Nayar below, "Request to Government on Kasturba's Funeral.")

a knack of surviving them and turning them into stepping-stones to success. Hence the saying peculiar to them that they blunder through to success. Failures do not dismay or demoralize them. They take them with calmness and in a sportsmanlike spirit. Wars are for them a national game like football. The defeated team heartily congratulates the successful one almost as if it was a joint victory, and drowns the sorrow of defeat in an exchange of glasses of whisky. If we have learnt nothing [of] worth from the contact with the British, let us at least learn their calmness in the face of misfortunes.

And is there the slightest cause for alarm? Certainly not for those who believe in non-violence. For fear and distrust of self are no part of their composition, nor are they part of a panoplied soldier. The attribute of non-violence is perhaps only a copy-book maxim. We do not see it in actual practice in any measure. But this war is abundant proof that neither party though steeped in violence betrays any fear or distrust.... This war is a demonstration of the unthinkable nerve that human beings are capable of possessing.

Looked at from either standpoint, therefore, we should be ashamed of fear, distrust and nervelessness in the face of danger. It is, therefore, the sacred duty of every worker to steel himself against cowardly panic and prevent its spread as far as he can. "Cowards die many times before their death." Let this not be proved of us.

The true danger exists only for cities. It may be very near due to the fall of Singapore and probable loss of Burma. One of the best precautions consists in those people who are not wanted in the cities or those who want to shun danger, migrating to the villages in an orderly manner. There should be no panicky rush. Those who must remain in the cities whether for business or otherwise should carry out instructions that may be issued by the authorities from time to time. Those who will not, for any reason whatsoever, should clear out in good time. If this simple precaution is taken, we may face the future without perturbation. More I cannot say, for we are a house divided against itself and there is no living bond between the rulers and the ruled. It is tragic but it is true. The tragedy is deepened by the knowledge that all parties feel so helpless.

In the next writing, Gandhi considers how India, as a nonviolent nation, should respond to the Japanese. Despite his idealism, he is a realist about the difficulties and length of the struggle. He seemingly shifts direction mid-way to talk about the Constructive Programme, which as he says, has always been the essential "best preparation" for nonviolence and independence. Bhikhu Parekh, in his book on Gandhi's life, work, and ideas, explains that "Gandhi worked out a comprehensive syllabus of national regeneration, which he appropriately called the Constructive Programme. Typically Gandhian in its content, it included both small and large items, covering different areas of life.... It included such 'absolutely essential' proposals as Hindu-Muslim unity, the removal of untouchability, a ban on alcohol, the use of khadi (hand-spun cloth), the development of village industries, and craft-based education" (7). In the following, Gandhi argues passionately for this vision of what the people of India need.

Non-Violent Resistance

On the Train to Wardha
April 5, 1942

Japan is knocking at our gates. What are we to do in a non-violent way? If we were a free country, things could be done non-violently to prevent the Japanese from entering the country. As it is, non-violent resistance could commence the moment they effected a landing. Thus non-violent resisters would refuse them any help, even water. For it is no part of their duty to help anyone to steal their country. But if a Japanese had missed his way and was dying of thirst and sought help as a human being, a non-violent resister, who may not regard anyone as his enemy, would give water to the thirsty one. Suppose the Japanese compel resisters to give them water, the resisters must die in the act of resistance. It is conceivable that they will exterminate all resisters. The underlying belief in such non-violent resistance is that the aggressor will, in time, be mentally and even physically tired of killing non-violent resisters. He will begin to search what this new (for him) force is which refuses co-operation without seeking to hurt, and will probably desist from further slaughter. But the resisters may find that the Japanese are utterly heartless and that they do not care how many they kill. The non-violent resisters will have won the day inasmuch as they will have preferred extermination to submission.

But things will not happen quite so simply as I have put them. There are at least four parties in the country. First the British and the army they have brought into being. The Japanese declare that they have no designs upon India. Their quarrel is only with the British. In this they are assisted by some Indians who are in Japan. It is difficult to guess how many, but there must be a fairly large number who believe in the declaration of the Japanese and think that they will deliver the country from the British yoke and retire. Even if the worst happens, their fatigue of the British yoke is so great that they would welcome the Japanese yoke for a change. This is the second party. The third are the neutrals, who though not non-violent will help neither the British nor the Japanese.

The fourth and last are non-violent resisters. If they are only a few, their resistance will be ineffective except as an example for the future. Such resisters will calmly die wherever they are but will not bend the knee before the aggressor. They will not be deceived by promises. They do not seek deliverance from the British yoke through the help of a third party. They believe implicitly in their own way of fighting and no other. Their light is on behalf of the dumb millions who do not perhaps know that there is such a thing as deliverance. They have neither hatred for the British nor love for the Japanese. They wish well to both as to all others. They would like both to do what is right. They believe that non-violence alone will lead men to do right under all circumstances. Therefore, if for want of enough companions non-violent resisters cannot reach the goal, they will not give up their way but pursue it to death.

The task before the votaries of non-violence is very difficult. But no difficulty can baffle men who have faith in their mission.

This is going to be a long drawn out agony. Let non-violent resisters not make impossible attempts. Their powers are limited. A resister in Kerala is not physically responsible for the defence of Assam which is just now in imminent danger. If Assam is non-violently inclined, it is well able to take care of itself. If it is not, no party of non-violent resisters from Kerala can help it or any other province. Kerala can help Assam etc. by demonstrating its non-violence in Kerala itself. The Japanese army, if it gets a foothold in India, will not stop at Assam. In order to defeat the British, it has to overrun the whole country. The British will fight every inch of the ground. Loss of India will probably be admission of complete defeat for them. But whether it is so or not, it is quite clear that Japan will not rest till India is wholly in her hands. Hence non-violent resisters must remain at their posts wherever they are.

One thing has to be made clear. Where the British army is actually engaging the 'enemy,' it would be perhaps improper for direct resistance to function. It will not be non-violent resistance when it is mixed with, it allies itself to, violence.

Let me therefore reiterate what I have said so often. The best preparation for, and even the expression of, non-violence lies in the determined pursuit of the constructive programme. Anyone who believes that without the backing of the constructive programme he will show non-violent strength when the testing time comes will fail miserably. It will be, like the attempt of a starving unarmed man to match his physical strength against a fully fed and panoplied soldier, foredoomed to failure. He who has no belief in the constructive programme has, in my opinion, no concrete feeling for the starved millions. He who is devoid of that feeling cannot fight non-violently. In actual practice the expansion of my non-violence has kept exact pace with that of my identification with starved humanity. I am still far from the non-violence of my conception, for am I not still far away from the identification of my conception with dumb humanity?

On July 14, 1942, the Congress Working Committee[91] *approved a resolution declaring "the immediate ending of the British rule in India," which became known as the "Quit India" resolution. The phrase had an electrifying effect on the nation. In May, Gandhi called on Britain to "leave India to God. If this is too much then leave her to anarchy" (www.gandhi-manibhavan.org). During the first week of August he and the Congress Working Committee labored together over the next steps to be taken. On August 9 he would address the All India Congress Committee with a speech that included these words: "Here is a mantra, a short one, that I give you. You may imprint it on*

91. The Congress Working Committee consisted of the senior party members of the Indian National Congress, also known as the Congress Party. The India National Congress is the "broadly based political party of India. Formed in 1885, the Indian National Congress dominated the Indian movement for independence from Great Britain and has formed most of India's governments from the time of independence" (www.britannica.com).

your hearts and let every breath of yours give expression to it. The mantra is: 'Do or Die.' We shall either free India or die in the attempt. ..." (CWMG-CD *83:197). "Do or Die" would also capture the imagination of the nation.*

It is in the context of this intense week that Gandhi writes to American friends to explain what must seem to Americans an unreasonable policy, a policy which will in a few days lead to Gandhi's imprisonment. He expresses his view of his celebrity status, criticisms of him, and his indebtedness to Thoreau, Ruskin, and Tolstoy

To American Friends

On Way to Bombay
August 3, 1942

Dear Friends,

As I am supposed to be the spirit behind the much discussed and equally well abused resolution of the Working Committee of the Indian National Congress on Independence, it has become necessary for me to explain my position. For I am not unknown to you. I have in America perhaps the largest number of friends in the West—not even excepting Great Britain. British friends knowing me personally are more discerning than the American. In America I suffer from the well known malady called hero worship. Good Dr. Holmes, until recently of the Unity Church of New York, without knowing me personally became my advertising agent. Some of the nice things he said about me I never knew myself. So I receive often embarrassing letters from America expecting me to perform miracles. Dr. Holmes was followed much later by the late Bishop Fisher who knew me personally in India. He very nearly dragged me to America but fates had ordained otherwise and I could not visit your vast and great country with its wonderful people.

Moreover, you have given me a teacher in Thoreau, who furnished me through his essay on the 'Duty of Civil Disobedience' scientific confirmation of what I was doing in South Africa. Great Britain gave me Ruskin, whose 'Unto This Last' transformed me overnight from a lawyer and city-dweller into a rustic living away from Durban on a farm, three miles from the nearest railway station and Russia gave me in Tolstoi, a teacher who furnished a reasoned basis for my non-violence. He blessed my movement in South Africa when it was still in its infancy, and of those wonderful possibilities I had yet to learn. It was he who had prophesied in his letter to me that I was leading a movement which was destined to bring a message of hope to the down-trodden people of the earth. So you will see that I have not approached the present task in any spirit of enmity to Great Britain and the West. After having imbibed and assimilated the message of 'Unto This Last,' I could not be guilty of approving Fascism or Nazism, whose cult is suppression of the individual and his liberty.

I invite you to read my formula of withdrawal or as it has been popularly called 'Quit India' with this background. You may not read into it more than the context warrants.

I claim to be a votary of truth from my childhood. It was the most natural thing to me. My prayerful search gave me the revealing maxim 'Truth is God' instead of the usual one 'God is Truth.' That maxim enables me to see God face to face as it were. I feel Him pervade every fibre of my being. With this Truth as witness between you and me, I assert that I would not have asked my country to invite Great Britain to withdraw her rule over India, irrespective of any demand to the contrary, if I had not seen at once that for the sake of Great Britain and the Allied cause it was necessary for Britain boldly to perform the duty of freeing India from bondage. Without this essential act of tardy justice, Britain could not justify her position before the unmurmuring World Conscience, which is there nevertheless. Singapore, Malaya and Burma taught me that the disaster must not be repeated in India. I make bold to say that it cannot be averted unless Britain trusts the people of India to use their liberty in favour of the Allied cause. By that supreme act of justice Britain would have taken away all cause for the seething discontent of India. She will turn the growing ill-will into active good-will. I submit that it is worth all the battleships and airships that your wonder-working engineers and financial resources can produce.

I know that interested propaganda has filled your ears and eyes with distorted versions of the Congress position. I have been painted as a hypocrite and enemy of Britain under disguise. My demonstrable spirit of accommodation has been described as my inconsistency, proving me to be an utterly unreliable man. I am not going to burden this letter with proof in support of my assertions. If the credit I have enjoyed in America will not stand me in good stead, nothing I may argue in self-defence will carry conviction against the formidable but false propaganda that has poisoned American ears.

You have made common cause with Great Britain. You cannot therefore disown responsibility for anything that her representatives do in India. You will do a grievous wrong to the Allied cause, if you do not sift the truth from the chaff while there is yet time. Just think of it. Is there anything wrong in the Congress demanding unconditional recognition of India's Independence? It is being said, 'But this is not the time.' We say, 'This is the psychological moment for that recognition. For then and then only can there be irresistable opposition to Japanese aggression. It is of immense value to the Allied cause if it is also of equal value to India. The Congress has anticipated and provided for every possible difficulty in the way of recognition. I want you to look upon the immediate recognition of India's Independence as a war measure of first class magnitude.

I am
Your Friend,
M. K. Gandhi

A week later, Gandhi was arrested.

Mahatmaji's Arrest

August 16, 1942

Gandhiji woke up as usual at 4 a.m. for the morning prayer today, Sunday the 9th instant. He was about to proceed with his daily routine after the prayers when the news came that the Police Commissioner was at the gate and wanted to see Mr. Mahadev Desai, Gandhiji's secretary. He brought with him warrants of arrest under the Defence of India Rules for Gandhiji, Mr. Mahadev Desai and Mirabehn (Miss Slade). There were no similar orders for Mrs. Gandhi and Pyarelal, Gandhiji's other Secretary, but the Police Commissioner said he had instructions to take them with Gandhiji under the same terms if they chose to accompany him. But they decided not to. In reply to Gandhiji's enquiry, the Police Commissioner informed Mr. Mahadev Desai that they had half an hour in which to get ready. Gandhiji had his breakfast of goat milk and fruit juice as usual. His favorite hymn

Vaishnav Jan was then sung by his party and the members of the Birla Family, his host. Verses from the Quran were recited by Amtulsalaam, a Muslim member of his Sevagram Ashram. He then left with a few personal belongings including his copy of Gita, Ashram hymn book, a copy of Quran, and Urdu Primer and his Dhanush-Takli for spinning. Before he boarded the car, he was garlanded and the auspicious Kum-Kum[92] mark was put on his forehead by Mrs. R.D. Birla, the hostess. Messrs. R.D. Birla, G.D. Birla[93] and other members of the family then bade farewell and he left with his usual smile accompanied by Mira Ben and the Police Commissioner in the front car, while Mr. Mahadev Desai followed him in the second car in charge of a Superintendent of Police.

Before Gandhiji left, Mr. G.D. Birla entreated him not to be in a hurry to go on fast. Gandhiji assured him that he would not do so precipitately. He was as a matter of fact trying to resist the idea of the fast. But if a clear call came from within requiring him to embark upon it, he would not be able to resist it.

This was the beginning of Gandhi's long imprisonment, lasting from August 1942 to May 1944. It was a tragic detention. Mahadev Desai and Kasturba, with Sushila Nayar as physician,[94] were also imprisoned in the Aga Khan Palace in Pune. In less than a week, Mahadev Desai died suddenly, probably of a stroke. Ba was ill almost from the beginning of the imprisonment. Her illness grew worse in spite of Sushila Nayar's efforts, and Ba died on February 22, 1944. Below is Gandhi's request for Ba's cremation. He put the request in terms of three alternatives stated in order of preference.

92. Kum-Kum: red powder (usually turmeric or saffron)

93. R.D. Birla (1892–1973) and G.D. Birla (1894–1983) were wealthy brothers, entrepreneurs and philanthropists who supported Gandhi.

94. Dr. Sushila Nayar (1914–2000) was the personal physician to Gandhi and Kasturba, and the younger sister of Pyarelal Nayar (see above, "Plea for Calmness").

Request to Government on Kasturba's Funeral

February 22, 1944

1. Body should be handed over to my sons and relatives which would mean a public funeral without interference from Government.

2. If that is not possible, funeral should take place as in the case of Mahadev Desai; and if the Government will allow relatives only to be present at the funeral, I shall not be able to accept the privilege unless all friends who are as good as relatives to me are also allowed to be present.

3. If this also is not acceptable to the Government, then those who have been allowed to visit her will be sent away by me and only those who are in the camp (detenus[95]) will attend the funeral.

It has been, as you will be able to bear witness, my great anxiety not to make any political capital out of this most trying illness of my life companion. But I have always wanted whatever the Government did, to be done with good grace which, I am afraid, has been hitherto lacking. It is not too much to expect that now that the patient is no more, whatever the Government decide about the funeral will be done with good grace.

Sushila Nayar, in Kasturba: Wife of Gandhi, *wrote this account of the government's response (69-71):*

... the Government were not prepared to allow a public funeral. A public funeral would have meant a big procession. It would have led to further awakening and enthusiasm amongst the people. How could they take such a risk? So they accepted the second alternative. ...

95. detenus: detainees

On the 23rd of February, friends and relatives started coming in from 7 a.m. There was a collection of about 150 people. Manu[96] offered "Arati" (worship with a light) to the body. Everyone made obeisance. There was a heap of floral offerings. Friends of every community—Hindus, Muslims, Parsis, Christians and Englishmen—were present. ...

After the body had been placed on the funeral pyre, Gandhiji offered a short prayer. It consisted of Hindu, Muslim, Christian and Parsi prayers. Devadasbhai[97] lighted the fire. ...

We took our floral offerings to the two samadhis[98] both morning and evening. In the morning we recited the 12th chapter of Gita. ...

Ba's illness had put tremendous strain on Gandhiji. His resistance had been lowered and as a result he went down with a severe attack of malaria. The Government was not prepared to take the responsibility of a third death in jail. On the 6th of May, the gates of the detention camp were thrown open and Gandhiji and his party were released.

After his release Gandhi returned to Sevagram, reaching there on August 3, 1944. The discussion which follows was with a young man who had been working in the villages. Gandhi, it appears, was pleased with the report.

---

96. Manu Gandhi (great-niece, Gandhi's uncle's great-granddaughter) was a nurse to Kasturba in her last illness and one of his inner circle and close aides in the last years. The summary of her account of his assassination is the last in this book. During the work in Noakhali (see below "A Letter from Gandhiji"), word got out and a scandal developed over Gandhi's practice of having Manu sleep by his side. Despite claims that this was part of Gandhi's brahmacharya and that there was "no trace of sexual arousal," Manu quit sleeping beside him; the scandal also was cause for the anthropologist Nirmal Kumar Bose to leave Gandhi's service (Tidrick 304-6, 312-13, 315; Rajmohan Gandhi 492-3, 548, 550-5).
97. Devadas, Gandhi and Kasturba's youngest son, lit the fire.
98. samadhis: those who have achieved the level of spiritual concentration just short of nirvana

Discussion with D. Ramaswami[99]

Sevagram
[August 3, 1944]

Re-organization of the villages is a very intricate problem, but if we can find even half a dozen workers of the right type, we can solve it in due time. The time factor is important, but given the right start the thing will grow like a snowball. You have heard of Booker T. Washington. We have to produce better workers than even him in order to achieve our object.

As for you, your ambition will be fulfilled if, besides your ability and enthusiasm, you introduce something else in your life, i.e., a living faith in God. Then all insipidity will vanish. A cosmopolitan outlook is a necessity but it can never be a substitute for God. God is there, but our conception of God is limited by our mental horizon and by our physical environment. For instance, when you read the Bible, you will find that the God of the Hebrews was quite different from the God of Jesus Christ. You are dissatisfied with the prevalent idea about God for the simple reason that those who profess belief in God do not present a living God in their own lives.

Unless you have a living faith in God to sustain you, when failure stares you in the face, there is disappointment for you. You may develop a revulsion for the work that you have taken up. You may begin to feel that after all what Dr. Ambedkar said was the right thing and you made a mistake in rejecting the high posts which you had been offered. My advice to you is that you should not leave this Ashram till you have found God. In spite of my limitless failings I am a seeker after Truth and so are my companions in this place. The Ashram, apart from its inhabitants, the sum total of energy that it represents, the principles for which it stands, may enable you to know God to the extent that you may be able to say 'God is,' just as you can say 'Truth is.'

Ramaswami: I can say that in the sense that Truth is the antithesis of falsehood.

99. "A young Harijan graduate who gave Gandhiji a report of his work in the villages and sought his help and guidance. Gandhiji was pleased with his report" (*CWMG-CD* 84:265n1).

Gandhiji: That is good enough. The seers have described God as "Neti, neti" ('Not this, not this'). Truth will elude you. The sum total of all that is true is Truth. But you can't sum up all that is true. Like most of those who have had Western education, you have got an analytical mind. But there are things that can't be analysed. God who can be analysed by my poor intellect won't satisfy me. Therefore I do not try to analyse Him. I go behind the relative to the absolute and I get my peace of mind. . . .

R.: I have carefully gone through your writings in *Harijan* and *Young India*. Your way of life appeals to me very much. It offers scope for the exercise of individual will. The idea of God introduces a determinism and that limits man. It interferes with his free will.

G.: Is there such a thing as free will? Where is it? We are mere playthings in the hands of Providence.

R.: What is the relationship between God and man, between Truth and God?

G.: I used to say 'God is Truth.' That did not completely satisfy me. So I said 'Truth is God.' He and His law are not different. God's law is God Himself. To interpret it man has to resort to intense prayer and merge himself in God. Each one will interpret the same in his or her own way. As for the relationship between man and God, man does not become man by virtue of having two hands. He becomes man by becoming a tabernacle of God. . . .

4.

Postwar Reconstruction

1946–1947

The War in Europe ended in the spring of 1945, and in August 1945 the war in Asia also ended, after the atomic bombings of Hiroshima and Nagasaki. In February 1946 Harijan *was revived, and Gandhi turned his attention to problems such as food shortages, the need to economize, and the need to share resources.*

He found time to write articles for Harijan *about topics that were dear to his heart. He saw opportunities to work on major parts of his vision for the nation, including the development of agriculture, village industries, natural health care, and institutions for nonviolent action, such as a non-violent volunteer corps. His life of prayer and his role as a spiritual leader became important to an ever-widening host of followers.*

But Indian independence was still being worked out and there was much to be done. The tensions between Hindus and Muslims grew worse. Violence erupted. Muslims massacred Hindus in Noakhali, Hindus massacred Muslims in Bihar, and rioting broke out in Calcutta. Gandhi was faced with doing all he could to reduce the growing violence and to maintain unity between Hindus and Muslims. Despite his own frailty, and against advice from aides and colleagues, he travelled to Calcutta and Noakhali to see what he could do. When he heard of the horrible violence in Bihar, he felt the need to go there as well, but learned that Nehru and Patel were going there. He was prepared to fast unto death if the Bihar violence did not cease (Rajmohan Gandhi 541-42).

What Ought to be Done

Sevagram
February 14, 1946

Food crisis should be regarded as a certainty. In the circumstances the following things should be attended to at once:

1. Every person should confine his daily wants regarding food to the minimum, consistent with his or her health requirements: and where, as in cities, milk, vegetables, oils and fruit are available, grains and pulses[100] should be reduced as they

100. pulses: peas or beans

easily can be. Starch can be derived from starchy roots such as carrots, parsnips, potatoes, yam, bananas; the idea being to exclude from present diet and conserve those grains and pulses which can be kept and stored. Vegetables too should not be eaten as an indulgence or for pleasure when millions are denied the use of these things altogether and are now threatened with starvation due to shortage of cereals and pulses.

2. Everyone who has access to any water should try himself or herself to grow some edible for personal or general use. The easiest way to do so is to collect clean earth, mix it with organic manure where possible—even a little bit of dried cow dung is good organic manure—and put it in any earthen or tin pot and throw some seeds of vegetables such as mustard and cress etc., and daily water the pots. They will be surprised how quickly the seeds sprout and give edible leaves which need not even be cooked but can be eaten in the form of a salad.

3. All flower gardens should be utilized for growing edibles. And in this connection I would suggest to the Viceroy, Governors and high officials to take the lead. I would ask the heads of agricultural departments at the Centre and Provinces to flood the country with leaflets in the provincial languages telling laymen how and what to grow easily.

4. Reduction should be taken up not merely the civilian population but equally, if not predominantly, by the military. I say predominantly for the military ranks being under rigid military discipline can easily carry out measures of economy. . . .

An article of the same date, written by H.N. Brailsford,[101] *quotes Gandhi and reports on what he is doing and saying, and also reports on new British policies, with the change of government in Britain: Churchill's Tories have been replaced by Labor, and Clement Attlee is the new Prime Minister.*

Gandhiji on New Spirit

[March 17, 1946]

When last I was in Poona, Gandhi was a prisoner and I was not allowed to meet him. Then, the town, gloomy and angry, was involved in a general strike. Today it is celebrating the spring carnival in a mood of gaiety.

Gandhi in his turn was happy when I met him, for Mr. Attlee's speech in the Indian debate had just opened the road to independence. He looked well and very much less than his age. He talked easily without a trace of tension. His manner was never solemn and often he relaxed in a humourous chuckle. In a way hard to define, one felt that this man was speaking for India. Though his moral stature lifts him high above the average man, he interprets what is typical and enduring in this nation's outlook. He warned me, none the less, that he would be speaking only for himself and not for the Congress.

Our talk took its start from the Prime Minister's recognition of India's right to choose independence. This, Gandhi welcomed, and not only this, but the whole tone of the speech. "But I can't forget," he went on, "that the story of Britain's connection with India is a tragedy of unfulfilled promises and disappointed hopes. We must keep an open mind. A seeker of truth will never begin by discounting his opponent's statement as unworthy of trust. So I am hopeful, and indeed, no responsible Indian feels otherwise. This time I believe that the British mean business. But the offer has come suddenly. Will India be jerked into independence? I feel today like a passenger who has been hoisted in a basket-chair on to a ship's deck in a stormy sea and has not yet found his feet. There should have been some psychological preparation, but even now it is not too late. The tide of bitterness had risen high and that is not good for the soul. The last two months should have been

101. Henry Noel Brailsford (1873–1958) was a left-wing journalist who had traveled to Soviet Russia, wrote numerous books, and contributed to periodicals such as *The New Statesman* (www.marxists.org).

filled with generous gestures. This is a milestone not only in India's history and Britain's, but in the history of the whole world."

Gandhi's meaning was clear. The British Government had done the right thing, but in its manner of doing it, he missed the big touch. When I asked him for concrete illustrations, he chose two. The release of the political prisoners had been gradual and was still incomplete. "There was no danger to fear. If independence is coming, would these men have opposed it? A complete amnesty would have captured the people's imagination. When you are about to transfer power, you should do it boldly."

He went on to speak of the salt tax. "Its abolition would be a gesture the poorest peasant could understand. It could mean even more to him than independence itself. Salt in this climate is a necessity of life, like air and water. He needs it for himself, his cattle, and his land. This monopoly will go the instant we get independence. Then why not abolish it today? By such acts the Government could have created a feeling among the masses that the new era has actually dawned...."

Gandhi now returns to an older idea, the development of a non-violent volunteer corps. Note that for Gandhi, these practical details are inseparable from faith.

Non-Violent Volunteer Corps

New Delhi
April 26, 1946

Some time ago an attempt was made, at my instance, to form shanti dals[102] but nothing came of it. This lesson, however, was learnt that the membership, in its very nature, of such organizations could not be large. Ordinarily, the efficient running of a large volunteer corps based on force implies the possibility of the use of force in the event of breach of discipline. In such bodies little or no stress is laid on a man's character. Physique is the chief factor. The contrary must obtain in non-violent bodies in which character or soul force

102. shanti dals: peace brigades

must mean everything and physique must take second place. It is difficult to find many such persons. That is why non-violent corps must be small, if they are to be efficient. Such brigades may be scattered all over; there may be one each for a village or a mohalla.[103] The members must know one another well. Each corps will select its own head. All the members will have the same status, but where everyone is doing the same work there must be one person under whose discipline all must come, or else the work will suffer. Where there are two or more brigades the leaders must consult among themselves and decide on a common line of action. In that way alone lies success.

If non-violent volunteer corps are formed on the above lines, they can easily stop trouble. These corps will not require all the physical training given in akhadas.[104] but a certain part of it will be necessary.

One thing, however, should be common to members of all such organizations and that is implicit faith in God. He is the only companion and doer. Without faith in Him these peace brigades will be lifeless. By whatever name one calls God, one must realize that one can only work through his strength. Such a man will never take another's life. He will allow himself, if need be, to be killed and thereby live through his victory over death.

The mind of the man in whose life the realization of this law has become a living reality will not be bewildered in crisis. He will instinctively know the right way to act.

In spite, however, of what I have said above I would like to give some rules culled from my own experience:

1. A volunteer may not carry any weapons.

2. The members of a corps must be easily recognizable.

3. Every volunteer must carry bandages, scissors, needle and thread, surgical knife etc. for rendering first aid.

4. He should know how to carry and remove the wounded.

---

103. mohalla: neighborhood

104. akhadas: training gyms

5. He should know how to put out fires, how to enter a fire area without getting burnt, how to climb heights for rescue work and descend safely with or without his charge.

6. He should be well acquainted with all the residents of his locality. This is a service in itself.

7. He should recite Ramanam[105] ceaselessly in his heart and persuade others who believe to do likewise.

There are many who, whether from mental laziness or from having fallen into a bad habit believe that God is and will help us unasked. Why then is it necessary to recite His name? It is true that if God is, He is irrespective of our belief. But realization of God is infinitely more than mere belief. That can come only by constant practice. This is true of all science. How much more true of the science of all sciences?

Man often repeats the name of God parrot-wise and expects fruit from so doing. The true seeker must have that living faith which will not only dispel the untruth of parrot-wise repetition from within him but also from the hearts of others.

Events are moving rapidly. In a later issue of Harijan, *Gandhi defines independence and also prints a press-summary of a speech by Churchill, who has been Gandhi's political opponent.*[106] *Despite Churchill's criticism of Gandhi and his adamant opposition to Indian independence, Gandhi expresses generosity towards him and makes a point of being optimistic. Churchill's*

---

105. Ramanam: devotional song; praise of Rama, here used as a mantra; see Ramanama

106. Winston Churchill (1874–1965) met Gandhi once, in London in 1906, when Churchill was Undersecretary for the Colonies while Gandhi was there lobbying on behalf of Indians in South Africa. Churchill refused to meet with him during the Round Table Conference in 1931, but he said to G.D. Birla, in 1935, that he admired Gandhi standing up for the untouchables. Churchill opposed Indian independence, throughout his years as Prime Minister, saying famously in 1942 he had "not become the King's First Minister in order to preside over the liquidation of the British Empire" (Rajmohan Gandhi 118, 436).

use of metaphor in the speech provides a contrast to the relative simplicity of emphasis in Gandhi's speeches.

Independence
April 29, 1946

Friends have repeatedly challenged me to define independence. At the risk of repetition, I must say that independence of my dream means Ramarajya,[107] i.e. the Kingdom of God on Earth. I do not know what it will be like in Heaven. I have no desire to know the distant scene. If the present is attractive enough, the future cannot be very unlike.

In concrete terms, then, the independence should be political, economic and moral.

'Political' necessarily means the removal of the control of the British army in every shape and form.

'Economic' means entire freedom from British capitalists and capital, as also their Indian counterpart. In other words, the humblest must feel equal to the tallest. This can take place only by capital or capitalists sharing their skill and capital with the lowliest and the least.

'Moral' means freedom from armed defence forces. My conception of Ramarajya excludes replacement of the British army by a national army of occupation. A country that is governed by even its national army can never be morally free and, therefore, its so-called weakest member can never rise to his full moral height.

Though Mr. Churchill is claimed to have won the war for the British, he has in his Aberdeen speech uttered words of wisdom from the standpoint of a radical non-violent reformer. He knows, if any panoplied warrior knows, what havoc the two wars of our generation have wrought. I reproduce the summary of his speech as reported in the public press. Only I must warn the public against the pessimistic note underlying the speech. Nothing will be found to have gone wrong if mankind recoils from the horrors of war. The bloodletting that men have undergone to the point of whiteness will

107. Ramarajya: the kingdom of Rama or the kingdom of God; wise governance; control of oneself by Rama dwelling in the heart itself is Rama's real kingdom (www.hindujagruti.org/hinduism).

not have been in vain, if it has taught us that we must freely give our own blood in the place of taking other peoples' blood, be the cause ever so noble or ignoble.

If the Cabinet Mission 'delivers the goods,' India will have to decide whether attempting to become a military power she would be content to become, at least for some years, a fifth-rate power in the world without a message in answer to the pessimism described above, or whether she will by further refining and continuing her non-violent policy prove herself worthy of being the first nation in the world using her hard-won freedom for the delivery of the earth from the burden which is crushing her in spite of the so-called victory.

The article of Gandhi's above is followed by the press summary of Churchill's speech.

Press Summary of Churchill's Speech

April 29, 1946

The world is very ill. This is the time when hatred is rife in the world and when many mighty branches of the human family, victors or vanquished, innocent or guilty, are plunged in bewilderment, distress or ruin. Two fearful wars in our lifetime have torn the heart out of its grace and culture.

Measureless injury has been done to much that the 19th century would have called 'Christian civilization,' for all the leading nations have been racked by stresses which have blunted their sensibilities and have destroyed their agreeable modes of social intercourse Only science has rolled forward, whipped by the fierce winds of mortal war, and science has placed in the hands of men agencies of destruction far beyond any development of their commonsense or virtue.

In a world where over-production of food was formerly from time to time a problem, famine has laid its gaunt fingers upon the peoples of many lands and scarcity upon all.

The psychic energies of mankind have been exhausted by the tribulations through which they have passed and are still passing. It is not only bloodletting that has weakened and whitened us.

The vital springs of human inspiration are, for the moment, drained. There must be a period of recovery. Mankind cannot, in its present plight, bear new shocks and quarrels without taking to altogether cruder and primordial forms.

Yet we do not know that the hatreds and confusion which are found will not confront us with even harder trial than those we have so narrowly and painfully survived.

In many countries, where even united efforts would fall short of what is needed, party strife and faction is fomented or machine-made and skeleton fanatics rave at each other about their rival ideologies.

All the while, the ordinary folk of every country show themselves kindly and brave and serviceable to their fellow men. Yet, they are driven against one another by forces and organizations and doctrines as wantonly and remorselessly as they ever were in the ages of absolute emperors and kings.

There never was a time when breathing space was more needed, a blessed convalescence, a truce of God and man.

In this post-war situation, Gandhi continues trying to formulate policies that will stop the violence which has broken out.

How Can Violence Be Stopped?

May 9, 1946

Q. Some time back a military officer in Poona, who [was] about to return to England, said to me that violence was on the increase in India and would further increase as people were gradually turning away from the path of non-violence. "We in the West" he said, "not only believe in violence but our society is based on it. Several subject races have won their independence through violence and are today living in peace. We have discovered the atom bomb for stopping violence. The last great war is a case in point." Continuing the military officer said, "Gandhiji has shown your people the way of non-violence. Has he discovered any such power as the atom bomb which will at once convert people to non-violence and bring about a rule of peace? Cannot Gandhiji's 'atom bomb' stop people from following the path of violence? Ask Gandhiji to exercise his power over the people and tell them to give up all thoughts of violence and adopt his creed. If he cannot wean his people today from the terrible violence that is spreading all over the country, I tell you that he will live a disappointed man and his life's work will be ruined."

A. There is much confusion of thought in this question. The atom bomb has not stopped violence. People's hearts are full of it and preparations for a third world war may even be said to be going on. While it would be absurd to say that violence has ever brought peace to mankind it cannot either be said that violence never achieves anything.

That I shall have to repent if I cannot stop violence does not enter into the picture of non-violence. No man can stop violence. God alone can do so. Men are but instruments in His hands. Here material means cannot stop violence but this does not mean that material means should not be employed for the purpose. The deciding factor is God's grace. He works according to His law and, therefore, violence will also be stopped in accordance with that law. Man does not and can never know God's law fully. Therefore we have to try as far as lies in our power. I hold that our experiment in non-violence has succeeded to a fair extent in India. There is, therefore, no room for the pessimism shown in the question. Finally Ahimsa is one of the world's great principles which no power on earth can wipe out. Thousands like myself may die in trying to vindicate the ideal but Ahimsa will never die. And the gospel of Ahimsa can be spread only through believers dying for the cause.

Gandhi continues to be questioned about the details of non-violence, in particular his ideas about the treatment of animals. In this reply Gandhi writes about realistic choices when confronted by violence, about cowardice and bravery and integrity.

Religion v. No Religion

May 29, 1946

A correspondent writes:

> ... You have written that your non-violence contemplates destruction of animals dangerous to mankind, such as leopards, wolves, snakes, scorpions, etc.

> You do not believe in giving food to dogs, etc. Several other people besides the Gujaratis look upon the feeding of dogs as a meritorious act. Such a belief may not be justifiable in times of food shortage like the present. Yet we must remember that these animals can be useful to man. One can feed them and take work out of them.

> You have put 27 questions to Shri Raichandbhai[108] from Durban. One of these questions was: "What should a seeker do when a snake attacks him?" His answer was: "He should not kill the snake and, if it bites, he should let it do so." How is it that you speak differently now?

I have written a lot on this subject in the past. At that time the topic was the killing of rabid dogs. There was much discussion on the subject but all that seems to have been forgotten.

My non-violence is not merely kindness to all living creatures. The emphasis laid on the sacredness of subhuman life in Jainism is understandable. But that can never mean that one is to be kind to this life in preference to human life. While writing about the sacredness of such life, I take it that the sacredness of human life has been taken for granted. The former has been over-emphasized. And, while putting it into practice, the idea has undergone distortion. For instance, there are many who derive complete satisfaction in feeding ants. It would appear that the theory has become a wooden, lifeless dogma. Hypocrisy and distortion are passing current under the name of religion.

---

108. Raychandbhai Ravajibhai Mehta (1867–1901) was a Jain philosopher and poet. In his *Autobiography*, Gandhi writes of being greatly helped by Raychandbhai. He was floundering as a young attorney, just returned from law school in London, when he met Raychandbhai who encouraged him to be patient and study Hinduism. Gandhi says that "three moderns have left a deep impress on my life"; these were Raychandbai, Tolstoy, and Ruskin (76-77, 120).

Ahimsa is the highest ideal. It is meant of the brave, never for the cowardly. To benefit by others' killing and delude oneself into the belief that one is being very religious and non-violent, is sheer self-deception.

A so-called votary of non-violence will not stay in a village, which is visited by a leopard every day. He will run away and when someone has killed the leopard, will return to take charge of his hearth and home. This is not non-violence. This is a coward's violence. The man who has killed the leopard has at least given proof of some bravery. The man who takes advantage of the killing is a coward. He can never expect to know true non-violence.

In life it is impossible to eschew violence completely. The question arises, where is one to draw the line? The line cannot be the same for everyone. Although essentially the principle is the same, yet everyone applies it in his or her own way. What is one man's food can be another man's poison. Meat-eating is a sin for me. Yet, for another person, who has always lived on meat and seen anything wrong in it, to give it up simply to copy me will be a sin.

If I wish to be an agriculturalist and stay in the jungle, I will have to use the minimum unavoidable violence in order to protect my fields. I will have to kill monkeys, birds and insects which eat up my crops. If I do not wish to do so myself, I will have to engage someone to do it for me. There is not much difference between the two. To allow crops to be eaten up by animals in the name of ahimsa while there is a famine in the land is certainly a sin. Evil and good are relative terms. What is good under certain conditions can become an evil or a sin under a different set of conditions.

Man is not to drown himself in the well of Shastras[109] but he is to dive into their broad ocean and bring out pearls. At every step he has to use discrimination as to what is ahimsa and what is himsa. In this there is no room for shame or cowardice. The poet has said that the road leading up to God is for the brave, never for the cowardly.

Finally, Raichandbhai's advice to me was that if I had courage, if I wanted to see God face to face, I should let myself be bitten by a snake instead of killing it. I have never killed a snake before or after receiving that letter. That is no matter of credit for me. My ideal is to be able to play with snakes and scorpions fearlessly. But it is merely a wish so far. Whether and when it will be realized I do not know. Everywhere I have let my people kill both. I

109. Shastras: religious treatises

could have prevented them if I had wished. But how could I? I did not have the courage to take them up with my own hands and teach my companions a lesson in fearlessness. I am ashamed that I could not do so. But my shame could not benefit them or me.

If Ramanama[110] favours me I might attain that courage some day. In the meantime, I consider it my duty to act as I have stated above. Religion is a thing to be lived. It is not mere sophistry.

Gandhi continues to get questions about religion, too, and he tries to answer them. In this reply, he expresses his faith in prayer and in God as an "all-pervading, all-embracing" force.

Is God A Person or a Principle?

Sevagram
August 8, 1946

A friend from Baroda writes in English:

> You ask us to pray to God to give light to the Whites in South Africa and strength and courage to the Indians to remain steadfast to the end. A prayer of this nature can only be addressed to a person. If God is an all-pervading and all-powerful force, what is the point of praying to Him? He goes on with his work whatever happens.

I have written on this topic before. But as it is a question that crops up again and again in different languages, further elucidation is likely to help someone or the other. In my opinion, Rama, Rahaman, Ahurmazda, God or

110. Ramanama: the chanting of the name Ram, the hero of the Ramayana. Here Gandhi appears to be referring to his devotion and faith.

Krishna[111] are all attempts on the part of man to name that invincible force which is the greatest of all forces. It is inherent in man, imperfect though he be, ceaselessly to strive after perfection. In the attempt he falls into reverie. And, just as a child tries to stand, falls down again and again and ultimately learns how to walk, even so man, with all his intelligence, is a mere infant as compared to the infinite and ageless God. This may appear to be an exaggeration but is not. Man can only describe in his own poor language. The power we call God defies description. Nor does that power stand in need of any human effort to describe Him. It is man who requires the means whereby he can describe that Power which is vaster than the ocean. If this premise is accepted, there is no need to ask why we pray. Man can only conceive God within the limitations of his own mind. If God is vast and boundless as the ocean, how can a tiny drop like man imagine what He is? He can only experience what the ocean is like, if he falls into it and is merged in it. This realisation is beyond description. In Madame Blavatsky's language man, in praying, worships his own glorified self.[112] He can truly pray who has the conviction that God is within him. He who has not, need not pray. God will not be offended, but I can say from experience that he who does not pray is certainly a loser. What matters then whether one man worships God as person and another as Force? Both do right according to their lights. None knows and perhaps never will know what is the absolutely proper way to pray. The ideal must always remain the ideal. One need only remember

111. Various names for God. Rama and Krishna are beloved Hindu deities, both of whom are avatars of Vishnu, one of the major deities, who pervades everything (*Hinduism: A Very Short Introduction* [Oxford UP], 124-26). Rahaman is a term from the Qur'an describing the nature of Allah; all but one chapter of the Qur'an begins with the words Bismillah ir-Rahman ir-Rahim, "In the name of God, most Gracious, most Compassionate" (http://wahiduddin.net/words/bismillah.htm). The 6th-century Persian prophet Zarathustra, founder of Zoroastrianism, believed he had seen visions of the supreme god Ahura Mazda; present day Parsis are believed to be descendants of Iranian Zoroastrians, who migrated to India in the 10th century (www.beliefnet.com; www.parsi.com).

112. Helena Blavatsky (1831–91) was a Theosophist, whom Gandhi met while in London studying law. He read her book *Key to Theosophy*, and, at a time when he was unsure about his own faith, he appreciated her sympathetic ideas about Hinduism, which missionaries had claimed was "rife with superstition" (*Autobiography* 60).

that God is the Force among all the forces. All other forces are material. But God is the vital force or spirit which is all-pervading, all-embracing and therefore beyond human ken.

Gandhi at the same time is ready to answer economic questions, especially questions about industrialization. He is not against technology as long as it is based on nonviolence and cooperation. He is against exploitation, imperialism, violence against the natural world, and the lack of restraint that detracts from living a moral life (Parekh 63-67). Near the end of his reply, Gandhi emphasizes his sense of universal humanity with an allusion to the song "For a' that" by Robert Burns.

Alternative to Industrialism

On the Train to Delhi
August 28, 1946

A correspondent writes:

> Do you then believe that industrialization of India—to the extent of India producing her own ships, locomotives, aeroplanes, etc.—is necessary? If not, will you kindly suggest the alternative means by which India shall discharge her responsibilities as a free and independent nation?" "If you believe in the establishment of such industries, who should, in your opinion, exercise control over the management and the profits that will accrue?

I do not believe that industrialization is necessary in any case for any country. It is much less so for India. Indeed, I believe that Independent India can only discharge her duty towards a groaning world by adopting a simple but ennobled life by developing her thousands of cottages and living at peace with the world. High thinking is inconsistent with complicated material life based on high speed imposed on us by Mammon worship. All the graces of life are possible only when we learn the art of living nobly.

There may be sensation in living dangerously. We must draw the distinction between living in the face of danger and living dangerously. A man who dares to live alone in a forest infested by wild beasts and wilder men without a gun and with God as his only Help, lives in the face of danger. A man who lives perpetually in mid-air and dives to the earth below to the admiration of a gaping world lives dangerously. One is a purposeful, the other a purposeless life.

Whether such plain living is possible for an isolated nation, however large geographically and numerically in the face of a world, armed to the teeth and in the midst of pomp and circumstance, is a question open to the doubt of the sceptic. The answer is straight and simple. If plain life is worth living, then the attempt is worth making even though, only an individual or a group makes the effort.

At the same time I believe that some key industries are necessary. I do not believe in arm chair or armed socialism. I believe in action according to my belief, without waiting for wholesale conversion. Hence, without having to enumerate key industries, I would have State ownership, where a large number of people have to work together. The ownership of the products of their labour, whether skilled or unskilled, will vest in them through the State. But as I can conceive such a State only based on non-violence, I would not dispossess monied men by force but would invite their co-operation in the process of conversion to State ownership. There are no pariahs of society, whether they are millionaires or paupers. The two are sores of the same disease. And all are men "for a' that."

And I avow this belief in the face of the inhumanities we have witnessed and may still have to witness in India as elsewhere. Let us live in the face of danger.

The following excerpt is quoted from an article printed in Harijan *with the title "Shrirampur Diary." The writer summarizes Gandhi's response to an American reading from a hymn by Isaac Watts.*

Shrirampur Diary

December 2, 1946

Two American friends who had come for relief work in Noakhali on behalf of the Friends Service Unit met Gandhiji just before prayers; and they remained over to pray with us. One of them, Prof. Stuart Nelson shared in it by reading out some words from Isaac Watts's famous hymn "Our God our help in ages past"; Gandhiji had originally intended to proceed further with explanation of the verses used in the Ashram prayer; but after Professor Nelson's recitation he preferred to explain the English hymn in Hindustani.

By way of introduction Gandhiji said that he felt very happy that Prof. Nelson had thus shared in the prayer. While in detention at the Aga Khan Palace, Mirabehn used to sing this hymn to him in her rich sonorous voice. He then paraphrased the meaning of the first three verses and said that the sentiment expressed in it was the same as found in the Gajendra moksha bhajan[113] sung last evening. There was the same reliance upon God, who was the source of all strength when every other earthly aid failed us. All human power was transient and real safety could lie only when we place our reliance wholly on God.

> Beneath the shadow of Thy throne
> Thy saints have dwelt serene:
> Sufficient is Thine arm alone
> And our defence is sure.

This is a lesson which all of us in Noakhali sorely needed to learn.

In this personal letter, Gandhi gives a picture of his peacemaking enterprise which shows it to be not merely his own action but the action of a number of individuals working on the same project. Narandas was Gandhi's nephew and Kanu, Gandhi's grand-nephew. Here Gandhi is writing to Narandas to tell him about the work of his "party" as they make there way in Bengal. He quotes from one of his favorite Christian hymns, "Lead, Kindly Light."

---

113. Gajendra moksha bhajan: section of the Gita telling of an elephant king

A Letter from Gandhiji

December 5, 1946

In the course of a letter to Shri Narandas Gandhi of Rajkot, Gandhiji writes:

"I have reverted to my usual diet and so there is no cause for worry. As a matter of fact, when a man leads a thoughtful life, there is no room for worry. My present mission is the most complicated and difficult one of my life. I can sing with cent per cent truth:

> The night is dark and I am far from home,
> Lead Thou me on.

I never experienced such darkness in my life before. The night seems to be pretty long. The only consolation is that I feel neither baffled, nor disappointed. I am prepared for any eventuality. 'Do or Die' has to be put to test here. 'Do' here means Hindus and Mussalmans should learn to live together in peace and amity. Otherwise, I should die in the attempt. It is really a difficult task. God's will be done.

All the companions have merged themselves into this sacred work quite willingly. If any one of them feels defeated, he or she is free to leave. Each one has chosen his or her own village. Each has with him a Bengali interpreter. Kanu (son of Narandas) also is posted in a village, different from that of Abha (Kanu's wife).[114] I am here in a remote and unhappy village. Parasuram could not be left alone on account of the difficulty of language. So he accompanies me. He is a silent worker and a very clever stenographer. My other companion is a Bengali professor. Both attend to my personal needs also. Most of the

114. Abha Gandhi (1927–95), wife of Kanu Gandhi (1917–86), was a close member of the inner circle; she was allowed to be with Kasturba during her final illness in the Aga Khan Palace, and became a part of Gandhi's team until his assassination. Abha worked with the support of Thakkar Bapa in Noakhali in the village of Haimchar to break down barriers between Hindus and Muslims. She and Manu (see above "Request ... On Kasturba's Funeral" and below "Manu Gandhi's Account") were often close to Gandhi providing support and aid (Rajmohan Gandhi 494, 547, 653-654). A photo of Abha, titled "Mrs. Kanu Gandhi" by Margaret Bourke-White was used as the cover of *Life* magazine, May 1, 1946 (www.life.com/image/50878472).

other companions are at a distance of ten miles from me. They can see me, when necessary. Pyarelal, Sushila Nayar and Sushila Pai[115] are in different villages. Kanu is quite happy and is carrying on Ramadhun. He has very regular habits, and is endowed by God with a good physique. Abba is with Thakkar Bapa. She is sixteen miles away. Bapa is taking keen interest in her. He is pleased with her spirit of service. She is preparing Gujarati chapatis[116] for him. Being a Bengali, she is able to do good work amongst Bengali women. She was extremely sorry to leave me. But duty lay that way. So I have kept her away from me. I must own that I was getting accustomed to her service almost as a matter of habit. But a habit of taking service from a particular individual is inconsistent with hard austerity. You will see thus, that whatever I do, I do from a sense of pure duty. You all should rejoice at this. Now, I have written long enough. You must all engross yourselves in your respective tasks.

With blessings,
Bapu

In response to the turmoil and bloodshed, Gandhi took up a new kind of Satyagraha. The bloody conflicts between Muslims and Hindus led him to go with some followers into the worst areas of conflict in East Bengal and live with a Muslim family if they would allow it. Gandhi's action of living with a Muslim family in Calcutta is pictured dramatically in the movie Gandhi, *but Gandhi had begun this kind of action several months earlier in East Bengal, which was torn by violence. Gandhi's strong protest began over forty years earlier when the British authorities divided Bengal into two parts on religious lines. The first of the three excerpts below was written by Pyrelal, the second is one of the daily reports on a regular prayer meeting, and the third is a personal report by Gandhi. What Gandhi is doing seems to be precursor of what later activists have called "accompanying," that is living with people who are involved in conflict situations, to protect them nonviolently, or working with them to help them control their own violent impulses.*

115. Sushila Pai, among Gandhi's "party" in Noakhali, "adopted" the village of Karpara for her own, eventually helping to reopen the local school and the weekly bazaar staying there to see what she could do (Rajmohan Gandhi 545, 558, 563).

116. chapattis (chapatis): flatbread

The "Do or Die" Mission

Kazirkhil
December 8, 1946

On the road to Satyagraha there is no stop. One must always move on and onward or else retrogress.... [Gandhi decided] he must live in a Muslim household, if a good Muslim Leaguer[117] approved of by the Bengal Ministry would be prepared to receive him as a member of the family. He discussed the question with Goffran Saheb, the Minister for Civil Supplies.... The latter was taken aback at Gandhiji's living stripped of all his companions in the midst of those who would not know how to look after him. "I shall look after myself. I shall need nobody's service," argued Gandhiji. "Then, I am afraid, I must say that no Mussalman family is prepared to receive you," replied Goffran Saheb laughing. But Gandhiji was not to be put away easily. He expatiated on it in his discourse after the evening prayer. He was in the midst of a Muslim population in Noakhali, he said. He did not like the idea of staying with Hindu friends. He would like to see if he could stay with a League Mussalman. "My requirements are very few. All I want is cleanliness, clean water, permissible food and the freedom to pray to God in my own way...."

But he did not want to postpone his new "Venture in Faith" till a Muslim household was ready to receive him. "When I was in detention in the Aga Khan Palace," he remarked one day, "I once sat down to write a thesis on India as a protagonist of non-violence. But as I proceeded with my writing I could not go on. I had to stop. There are two aspects of Hinduism. There is on the one hand the historical Hinduism with its untouchability, superstitious worship of stocks and stones, animal sacrifice and so on. On the other, we have the Hinduism of the Gita, the Upanishads and Patanjali's Yoga Sutra which is the acme of ahimsa and oneness of all creation, pure worship of one immanent, formless, imperishable God. Ahimsa which to me is the chief glory of Hinduism has been sought to be explained away by our people as being meant for sannyasis[118] only. I do not share that view.

---

117. Gandhi felt it essential to live with a member of the Muslim League to demonstrate the unity and understanding that he had long advocated.

118. sannyasis: monks, hermits, ascetics

I have held that it is the way of life and India has to show it to the world. Where do I stand? Do I represent this ahimsa in my person? If I do, then deceit and hatred that poison the atmosphere should dissolve. It is only by going into isolation from my companions, those on whose help I have relied all along, and standing on my own crutches that I shall find my bearings and also test my faith in God."

To Sevagram Ashram people he wrote:

"I am afraid you must give up all hope of my early returning or returning at all to the Ashram. The same applies to my companions. It is a herculean task that faces me. I am being tested. Is the Satyagraha of my conception a weapon of the weak or really that of strong? I must either realize the latter or lay down my life in the attempt to attain it. That is my quest. In pursuit of it I have come to bury myself in this devastated village. His will be done." ...

The hut where he was put up in Shrirampur is in an open sunny clearing in the midst of thick groves of stately arecanut and cocoanut palms. Round about it is spread a grim scene of arson and devastation. He has given up his warm immersion bath and for the first two days did his own massage. Since his arrival he has had several meetings with Shamsuddin Saheb[119] and others and a conference with about 30 representatives of Hindus and Muslims of Ramganj at Ramganj. As a result they were able to evolve a plan for the re-establishment of peace and communal harmony. The Ministers gave a solemn word of honour that they meant to implement it. The plan was put before the public at a public meeting that was held in the village of Chandipur on the 23rd November.

Gandhi speaking at the close of the meeting uttered the following words:

"Here are elected Muslims who are running the Government of the Province. They have given you their word of honour. They would not be silent witnesses to the repetition of shameful deeds. My advice to the Hindus

119. Shamsuddin Saheb: Bengal's minister for commerce (Rajmohan Gandhi 543)

is to believe their word and give them a trial. This does not mean that there would not be a single bad Mussalman left in East Bengal. There are good and bad men amongst all communities. Dishonourable conduct could break any Ministry or organization in the end.... If you want real peace there is no other way except to have mutual trust and confidence. Bihar, they say, has avenged Noakhali. Supposing the Muslims of East Bengal or the Muslims all over India make up their minds to avenge Bihar, where would India be?... After all if the worst came to the worst, you can only lose your lives. Only, you must do so as brave men and women.... If Shamsuddin Saheb and his companions do not mean what they have said, you will know. I for one would not wish to be a living witness to such a tragedy."

5.

Last Months

1947–1948

The selections that follow are remarkable for their expression of Gandhi's ideas on religion, economics, and nonviolent political action, which have largely merged in Gandhi's thinking.

In August 1947, the hope of independence for the people of India was realized. Independence was granted without the violent overthrow of government that has accompanied most independence movements. It was a triumph for nonviolence, a triumph for Gandhi and for satyagraha. Much of what happened leading up to independence was the result of a whole range of political changes in the world, and especially in Britain. Shortly after the end of the war in 1945, there was a political shift in Britain. Churchill's Conservative Party was defeated, and a Labor Government under Clement Attlee which supported Indian independence came to power. Lord Mountbatten became Governor General of India with the understanding that he would oversee the transition to independence. On August 15, 1947, two years after the end of World War II, India became an independent nation, with Jawaharlal Nehru as Prime Minister.

Gandhi had failed, however, after decades of work, to establish Hindu-Muslim cooperation and unity. The independence of India was followed by the establishment of two states, India, which was actually a secular state (with a large Hindu majority), and Pakistan, which was heavily Muslim. This division of India was accompanied by extreme communal violence and a massive refugee problem, with Muslims moving to Pakistan, and Hindus moving from Pakistan to India. This division of the sub-continent of India produced territorial disputes that still plague the area to this day. Much of what follows in the text of this chapter has to do with Gandhi's efforts to stop the communal violence.

Gandhi had also worked to integrate untouchables and lower-caste Hindus into the Hindu community. But in the end, the untouchables, under the leadership of Dr. Ambedkar, rejected Gandhi's idea of the integration of untouchables into the body of Hinduism, and opted for continued separation, with a quota system that would ensure proportional representation in schools and colleges and in legislative bodies. They rejected the term "Harijan," preferring "Dalit," meaning "the oppressed," and encouraged conversions to other religions, including Christianity and Buddhism.

Under Jawaharlal Nehru's leadership as India's first prime minister, Gandhi's ideas on economics were also rejected. Gandhi's vision was of a country of relatively self-sufficient villages. Gandhi had opposed both capitalism and socialism, and argued for a decentralized economy. His efforts to promote the spinning wheel—not only as a symbol of self-reliance, but also as a practical means of achieving economic independence for India's millions—were not accepted by the country as a whole. Nehru's government leaned toward a large-scale planned economy, and initiated a series of Soviet-style five-year plans. Some efforts toward the Gandhian economy were carried on under Vinoba Bhave and Jayaprakash Narayan. These efforts are significant and important but in a country with a billion people they may seem minuscule. Today, relatively few apparently see themselves as following in Gandhi's steps, but their efforts continue and are recognized in books from India and the West such as Rajni Bakshi's Bapu Kuti, *David Cortright's* Gandhi and Beyond, *Catherine Ingram's* In the Footsteps of Gandhi, *and Mark Juergensmeyer's* Gandhi's Way: A Handbook of Conflict Resolution.

In addition to the issues above, the selections in this section offer insights into Gandhi's thoughts and emotions during this last period in his life. Finally, this chapter provides accounts of Gandhi's last week, his state of mind, and the circumstances surrounding his assassination.

Personal Writings

The following brief but very personal letter provides insight into Gandhi's beliefs about life and death. Amiya Chakravarty,[120] *a younger friend, was literary secretary to Rabindranath Tagore and walked with Gandhi in the Salt March of 1930.*

Letter to Amiya Chakravarty

August 11, 1947

My Dear Amiya,

120. Amiya Chakravarty (1901–86) served as a secretary to Rabindranath Tagore and was a professor at Calcutta University. He taught at Selly Oak College, Birmingham, advised the Indian delegation to the United Nations, in 1948 joined the English department at Howard University, and later became a professor at Boston University (http://en.academic.ru).

I am sorry for your loss which in reality is no loss. Death is but a sleep and a forgetting. This is such a sweet sleep that the body has not to wake again and the dead load of memory is thrown overboard. So far as I know, happily there is no meeting in the beyond as we have it today. When the isolated drops melt, they share the majesty of the Ocean to which they belong. In isolation they die but to meet the Ocean again. I do not know whether I have been clear enough to give you any comfort.

Love
Bapu

On August 26, Mountbatten had written: "In the Punjab we have 55 thousand soldiers and large-scale rioting is on our hands. In Bengal our forces consist of one man, and there is no rioting. As a serving officer, as well as an adminstrator, may I be allowed to pay my tribute to the One-man Boundary Force, not forgetting his Second in Command, Mr. Suhrawardy" (CWMG-CD *96:303n1). Shaheed Suhrawardy was the Bengal premier who belonged to the Muslim League, with whom Gandhi stayed while he was trying successfully to end the communal violence in Calcutta.*[121] *The letter reveals the cordial, warm friendship and respect between Gandhi and Lord Mountbatten.*

Letter to Lord Mountbatten

Calcutta
August 30, 1947

Dear Friend,

Many thanks for your letter which His Excellency the Governor sent me yesterday afternoon. I do not know if Shaheed Sahib and I can legitimately appropriate the compliment you pay us. Probably suitable conditions

121. Hasan Shaheed Suhrawardy (1892–1963) urged Gandhi to come directly to Calcutta, which needed his aid. He assured Gandhi that attacks on Hindus in Noakhali would be prevented, and he arranged for a special train for Gandhi to make the journey (Rajmohan Gandhi 541-43).

were ready for us to take the credit for what appears to have been a magical performance.

Am I right in gathering from your letter that you would like me to try the same thing for the Punjab? I am in correspondence with the Pandit and the Sardar.[122] I hope your new office [as Governor General of independent India] is not unduly more arduous than as Viceroy.

It filled me with joy when I read in the papers that Lady Mountbatten had flown to the Punjab. I hope she is none the worse for the trying visit.

Yours sincerely.
M. K. Gandhi

This selection was not written by Gandhi, but is a report of an event that shows Gandhi's state of mind on this, his last birthday.

Note on Gandhiji's 78th Birthday

October 1947

The second of October 1947 was Gandhiji's birthday—the last to be celebrated in his lifetime. Members of his party came in the early morning to offer him their obeisances. "Bapuji", one of them remarked, "on our birthdays, it is we who touch the feet of other people and take their blessings but in your case it is the other way about. Is this fair?"

Gandhiji laughed: "The ways of Mahatmas are different! It is not my fault. You made me Mahatma, maybe a bogus one; so you must pay the penalty!"

He observed this birthday, as usual, by fasting, prayer and extra spinning. The fast, he explained was for self-purification, and the spinning a token of the renewal of his covenant to dedicate his being to the service of the lowliest and the least in God's creation. He had turned his birthday

122. "The Pandit" and "the Sardar" refer here to Jawaharlal Nehru and Vallabhbhai Patel. Literally, a Pandit is one who has memorized large portions of the Vedas, usually a Brahmin. The word is the origin of the English "pundit." Sardar means political leader or commander.

celebration into a celebration of the rebirth of the spinning-wheel. It stood for non-violence. The symbol appeared to have been lost. But he had not stopped the observance hoping that there might be at least a few scattered individuals true to the message of the wheel. It was for their sake that he allowed the celebration to continue.

A small party of intimate friends was waiting for him when he entered his room after his bath at half past eight. They included Pandit Nehru and the Sardar, G.D. Birla—his host—and all the members of the Birla family in Delhi. Mirabehn had gaily decorated his seat by improvising in front of it an artistic cross, He Rama and the sacred syllable Om from flowers of variegated colors. A short prayer was held in which all joined. It was followed by the singing of his favourite hymn "When I survey the wondrous Cross" and another devotional hymn of his choice in Hindi—He Govinda rakho sharan.

Visitors and friends continued to come all day to offer homage to the Father of the Nation. So also came the members of the Diplomatic Corps, some of them with greetings from their respective Governments. Lastly Lady Mountbatten arrived with a sheaf of letters and telegrams addressed to him.

His request to all was to pray that "either the present conflagration should end or He should take me away. I do not wish another birthday to overtake me in an India still in flames."

"What sin must I have committed," he remarked to the Sardar, "that He should have kept me alive to witness all these horrors?"

He seemed to be consumed by the feeling of helplessness in the face of the surrounding conflagration. Recorded the Sardar's daughter, Manibehn, mournfully that day in her journal: "His anguish was unbearable. We had gone to him in elation; we returned home with a heavy heart."

After the visitors had left, he had another spasm of coughing. "I would prefer to quit this frame unless the all-healing efficacy of His name fills me," he murmured. "The desire to live for 125 years has completely vanished as a result of this continued fratricide. I do not want to be a helpless witness of it."

"So from 125 years you have come down to zero," someone put in.

"Yes, unless the conflagration ceases. ..."

The All-India Radio had arranged a special broadcast programme in observance of his birthday. Would he not, for that once, listen to the special programme?—he was asked. "No," he replied; he preferred rentio (spinning wheel) to radio. The hum of the spinning-wheel was sweeter. He heard in it the "still sad music of humanity."

Gandhiji refused to release for publication any of the birthday messages—telegrams or letters—which had come from all parts of the world. He had many beautiful messages from Muslim friends, too, but he felt that it was no time for their publication when the general public seemed to have ceased, for the time being at least, to believe in non-violence and truth.

This selection is a striking expression of Gandhi's friendly relations with the Mountbattens and with the royal family. The Prince Consort who was marrying Princess Elizabeth was Lord Mountbatten's nephew Phillip. The gift was a piece of handmade table linen. A note in the text says that "Lord and Lady Mountbatten personally delivered the gift to Princess Elizabeth. It was prominently exhibited among the wedding gifts at St. James." On his return Lord Mountbatten conveyed to Gandhiji a personal message of appreciation and thanks from the Princess and the Prince consort. The Princess, Mountbatten reported, was extremely touched that Gandhiji should have made this very fine gesture to them and she said that she always intended to keep it in a place of safety as a precious souvenir and not to use it as a tea-cloth as she valued its historic association" (CWMG-CD *97:265n5). To this day, the tea-cloth is preserved in the royal collections.*

Letter to Lord Mountbatten

Birla House, New Delhi
November 9, 1947

Dear Lord Mountbatten,

This little thing is made out of doubled yarn of my own spinning. The knitting was done by a Punjabi girl who was trained by Abha's husband, my grandson. Lady Mountbatten knows Abha. Please give the bride and the bridegroom this with my blessings, with the wish that they would have a long and happy life of service of men.

I hope you will have a happy time and safe return according to your timetable.

Yours sincerely,
M. K. Gandhi

In these last months there are almost daily reports of what Gandhi said at a Prayer Meeting. In this speech Gandhi compares the current struggles to the accounts in the ancient Hindu epic, the Ramayana, of the struggle between the Hindu god, Rama, and Ravana, who is a personification of evil. This speech is significant for the expression of Gandhi's belief that social transformation must be preceded by the internal transformation of the heart. He has faith in a universal power of inward spiritual love, found too in the "Sermon on the Mount" and in the Quaker belief in following the leadings of the inward light. It may be that his lifelong practice of writing newspaper columns had evolved into these published prayer meeting messages.

Speech at Prayer Meeting

November 12, 1947

Brothers and Sisters,

Today is Diwali[123] and I congratulate all of you on the occasion. It is a great day in the Hindu calendar. According to the Vikram Samvat,[124] New Year begins tomorrow on Thursday. You must understand why Diwali is celebrated every year with illuminations. In the great battle between Rama and Ravana, Rama symbolized the forces of good and Ravana the forces of evil. Rama conquered Ravana and this victory established Ramarajya in India.

But alas! There is no Ramarajya in India. So how can we celebrate Diwali? Only those who have Rama within can celebrate this victory. For God alone can illumine our souls and only that light is the real light.... Crowds of people go to see artificial illumination but what we need today is the light of love in our hearts. We must kindle the light of love within. Then only would we deserve congratulations. Today thousands are in acute distress.

123. Diwali: festival of lights and the renewal of life

124. Vikram Samvat: popular Hindu lunar calendar

Can you, everyone of you, lay your hand on your heart and say that every sufferer, whether Hindu, Sikh or Muslim, is your own brother or sister? This is the test for you. Rama and Ravana are symbols of the unending struggle between the forces of good and evil. True light comes from within. ...

It is the duty of everyone to banish hatred and suspicion from his heart in order to establish peace and goodwill in the country. If you do not feel the presence of God within you and do not forget your petty internal quarrels, success in Kashmir or Junagadh would prove futile. Diwali cannot be celebrated till you bring back all the Muslims who have fled in fear. Pakistan also would not survive if it does not do likewise with the Hindus and Sikhs who have run away from there.

Tomorrow I shall tell you what I can about the Congress Working Committee. May you and all India be happy in the new year which begins on Thursday. May God illumine your hearts so that you can serve not only each other or India but the whole world.

In this selection Gandhi turns to one of his major concerns, the establishment of village industries. He still sees the economic future of India in a decentralized economy, neither communist, nor socialist, nor capitalist—an economy which will make it possible for people to support themselves and provide for the needs of each other through their own efforts. One might wonder whether we are now further from Gandhi's ideal than people were then. On the other hand, something very like the Gandhi ideal is now being carried out in micro-lending and similar self-help programs—many of them run by women—in many villages and even cities of India.

A Note [to a Member of the All India Village Industries Association[125]]

November 17, 1947

I find that talk of khadi and village industries does not interest people any more. Here I am sitting in the capital. Refugees are lying around shelterless and shivering. Thousands are pouring in every day. How long will you feed them without giving them any work? I am sure everyone will remember this old man one day when it is realized that India has no alternative except to develop village industries. Any government formed by any party—Congress, Socialist or Communist—will be forced to accept this truth. We do not realize this today, but we shall realize it after we stumble in our attempts to compete with America or Russia.

This talk was in answer to a friend who was accompanying Nehru and had asked Gandhi how peace in the world was to be established. As with the previous selection, Gandhi's comments here express his sense of the interconnectedness of religious faith, concern for the poor as well as the rich, and nonviolent social action. Gandhi sees the profound connection between affluence and the desire for luxuries and the causes of war.

A Talk

New Delhi

December 5, 1947

... one must first look deeply into the causes of wars and seek ways to remove those causes. Wars in a large measure are fought over economic issues. If we give up selfishness and resolve to take the barest minimum for the satisfaction of our wants, there will be no occasion for wars. Unless there

125. Gandhi and his close associate J.C. Kumarappa, an economist, in 1934 founded the All India Village Industries Association at Wardha. Through this organization, Gandhi "started experiments in rural life-style such as revival of village crafts and agro processing industries, village cleanliness, diet reforms, etc., so that villages could be developed as ideal surroundings to live in" (www.gandhi-manibhavan.org).

is a complete transformation in our economy and our style of life, peace will elude us, however hard we may strive for it. Europe and America want peace and yet they use their intellectual, technical and scientific resources for production of nuclear weapons. Therefore, while they express the wish that peace should reign in the world, they are busy inventing ways to disturb the peace and to destroy the world. It does not occur to them to seek ways to restore peace and stop the possibility of wars.

Last Fast and Death

The selections below all relate to Gandhi's last fast, which was carried out at Birla House in New Delhi as Gandhi's final effort to persuade Hindus and Muslims to stop killing each other. Gandhi had employed fasting on at least fourteen previous occasions, for a variety of reasons. Fasting was always a very controversial action. It had been successful for Gandhi many times. This time Gandhi was probably at the greatest risk, because of his age and the state of his health.

Personal Messages

> *From the month before starting the fast, until he ended it, Gandhi provided many brief personal messages. The first appeared in* Harijan *on December 10 under the heading 'Question Box.'*

Such a question has been put to me before but never perhaps precisely in the same terms. The answer, however, is easy. It is the last weapon in the armoury of the votary of ahimsa. When human ingenuity fails, the votary fasts. This fasting quickens the spirit of prayer, that is to say, the fasting is a spiritual act and, therefore, addressed to God. The effect of such action on the life of the people is that when the person fasting is at all known to them their sleeping conscience is awakened. But there is the danger that the people through mistaken sympathy may act against their will in order to save the life of the loved one. This danger has got to be faced. One ought not to be deterred from right action when one is sure of the rightness. It can but promote circumspection ... a fast is undertaken in obedience to the dictates of the inner voice and, therefore, prevents haste.

This statement, dated January 13, is from a talk to a Sikh friend:

My fast is against no one party, group or individual exclusively and yet it excludes nobody. It is addressed to the conscience of all, even the majority community in the other Dominion. If all or any one of the groups responds fully, I know the miracle will be achieved. For instance, if the Sikhs respond to my appeal as one man, I shall be wholly satisfied. I shall go and live in their midst in the Punjab, for they are a brave people, and I know they can set an example in non-violence of the brave which will serve as an object lesson to all the rest. ...

The next, also written on January 13, is from Gandhi's talk to a Prayer Meeting:

... I shall terminate the fast only when peace has returned to Delhi. If peace is restored to Delhi it will have effect not only on the whole of India but also on Pakistan and when that happens, a Muslim can walk around in the city all by himself. I shall then terminate the fast. ...

So my wish is that Hindus, Sikhs, Parsis, Christians and Muslims who are in India should continue to live in India and India should become a country where everyone's life and property are safe. Only then will India progress.

The next day, January 14, he wrote a letter to his own people, Gujaratis.

... I do not consider this an ordinary fast. I have undertaken it after much reflection. Yet it is not reflection that has impelled it; it is God who rules over reason. It is addressed to no one or addressed to all. There is no anger of any kind behind it, nor the slightest tinge of impatience. There is a time for everything. Of what use would any efforts be after the opportunity has slipped? …

On January 15, Gandhi spoke the following in Prayer Meeting, as he lay in bed at Birla House because of increasing weakness. He spoke these two paragraphs into a microphone. The remainder of the letter, which is not included here, was dictated earlier (CWMG-CD *98:326n1).*

Brothers and Sisters:

This is a new experience for me. I have never so far had occasion to convey my word thus to the people. I cannot go to the prayer ground and my voice from here cannot reach you. Even so I thought that if you could hear my voice you would feel reassured. … I do not know for how long this state will continue.

My request to you is that none of you should think what another is doing, but each of you should examine your own self and purify yourself to the extent you can. I am convinced that if people in large numbers purify themselves it will do them a lot of good and it will also do me good. India then will benefit and maybe I shall be able to give up the fast sooner. Let no one be concerned about me. Let everyone be concerned for himself. You must give thought to the progress of the country and the welfare of the people. In the end all men have to die. He who is born cannot escape death. Why then should we fear death or grieve over it? It is my belief that death is a friend to whom we should be grateful, for it frees us from the manifold ills which are our lot.

The next day, January 16, he wrote to Mirabehn. It is apparent that the fast was begun with a Prayer Meeting. The hymn referred to was "When I Survey the Wondrous Cross," which was a favorite Christian hymn for Gandhi. The choice is interesting since Gandhi is about to take an action which may result in his death. Also, it is important to note that he speaks of the fast more as a spiritual act of worth in itself than as a means of achieving results.

Dear Mira:

I got your letter yesterday. Evidently when you wrote it, you had no knowledge of this, my greatest fast. Whether it will ultimately prove so or not is neither your concern nor mine. Our concern is the act itself, not the result of the action. The fast was commenced as usual with a service, part of which was singing of "When I survey."[126] It was well sung by Sushila. There were some good friends at the service. The company was impromptu. No one was invited. I am dictating this immediately after the 3.30 a.m. prayer. …

Don't rush here because I am fasting. The yajna,[127] as I have called it, demands that everyone, wherever he or she is, should perform his or her duty. If an appreciable number do this, I must survive the ordeal. Trust God and be where you are. …

Also on January 16, Gandhi managed to speak at Prayer Meeting.

Brothers and Sisters,

I had not hoped to be able to speak to you today. But you will be glad to know that by God's grace I feel my voice is stronger than it was yesterday. During all my previous fasts I never felt as strong as I am feeling today: My hope is that if you will continue the yajna of self-purification my strength to address you can remain to the end. I may say that I am in no hurry at all. Hurry will not help our work. I feel ineffable peace. I do not want that anyone should do anything incompletely and tell me that everything is all right. When there is perfect peace in Delhi, there will be peace all over India. I have no wish to live if I cannot see peace established all round me, in India as well as in Pakistan. This is the meaning of this yajna. …

126. Isaac Watts' hymn "When I Survey the Wondrous Cross"

127. yajna: ritual

In this speech at Prayer Meeting on January 17, he is much weaker and has dictated his message.[128] *Note that Gandhi is adhering to principles, such as the essential importance of "humility," expressed over twenty years earlier in the* Autobiography.

Brothers and Sisters,

God's mercy it is that on this fifth day of the fast I can speak a few words without feeling exhausted. I have dictated the message for today which Sushilabehn will read out to you.

Whatever you do words must be backed by your full mind and heart, or it will avail nothing. You will be making the greatest mistake if you think only of how I am to be kept alive. It is not in any human hand to keep me alive or to kill me. It is in God's hands. I have not the least doubt about it, and no one else should have the least doubt.

The meaning of this fast is that our hearts should be cleansed and awakened. In that alone lies the good of all. Please do nothing out of pity for me. I shall last for as many days as I can and if it is the will of God that I should die then I shall die.

I know many of my friends are distressed and want me to terminate the fast at once. Today I cannot do so. When the occasion for it comes I shall not persist in the fast. Ahimsa requires us to accept our limitations and not to feel proud. It calls for humility. There is no pride in what I say. There is only pure love in it.

Gandhi broke his fast on January 18. Over a hundred representatives of various groups and organizations in Delhi called on Gandhi at 11:30 a.m. with a seven point declaration, beginning "We wish to announce that it is our heartfelt desire that the Hindus, Muslims and Sikhs and members of other communities should once again live in Delhi like brothers and we take the pledge that we shall protect the life, property and faith of Muslims and that the incidents which have taken place in Delhi will not happen again. … We assure that all these things will be done by our personal effort and not with

128. "Lying in bed Gandhiji spoke this in Hindi on the microphone" (*CWMG-CD* 98:245n1).

the help of the police or military. We request Mahatmaji to believe us and to give up his fast and to continue to lead us as he has done hitherto."

Gandhi replied:

... I am happy to hear what you have told me, but if you have overlooked one point all this will be worth nothing. If this declaration means that you will safeguard Delhi and whatever happens outside Delhi will be no concern of yours, you will be committing a grave error and it will be sheer foolishness on my part to break my fast. ...

Delhi is the heart—the capital of India. The leaders from the whole of India have assembled here. Men have become beasts. But if those who have assembled here, who constitute the cream among men cannot make the whole of India understand that Hindus, Muslims and followers of other religions are like brothers, it bodes ill for both the Dominions. What will be the fate of India if we continue to quarrel with one another? ... [Here Gandhi broke down from exhaustion, and the rest of his speech was read. The last paragraph reads:] After listening to all that I have said, if you still ask me to end my fast I shall end it. Afterwards you have to release me. I had taken the vow to do or die in Delhi and now if I am able to achieve success here I shall go to Pakistan and try to make Muslims understand their folly. Whatever happens in other places, people in Delhi should maintain peace. The refugees here should realize that they have to welcome as brothers the Muslims returning from Pakistan to Delhi. The Muslim refugees in Pakistan are suffering acute hardships and so are the Hindu refugees here. Hindus have not learnt all the crafts of Muslim craftsmen. Therefore they had better return to India. There are good men as well as bad men in all the communities. Taking into consideration all these implications, if you ask me to break my fast I shall abide by your wish. India will virtually become a prison if the present conditions continue. It may be better if you allow me to continue my fast and if God wills it He will call me. ...

There were positive responses from Hindu and Muslim leaders.

I shall break my fast. Let God's will prevail. You all be witness today.

Gandhi's decision was followed by recitations from Hindu, Buddhist, Islamic, and Parsi scriptures and singing of a Christian hymn. Abdul Azad, a Muslim leader, offered Gandhi a glass of juice, and Gandhi broke his fast.

The following statement, four days before Gandhi's assassination, gives some insight into Gandhi's state of mind. After having escaped a failed assassination attempt that used a bomb, Gandhi is reflecting on his own humanity as well as on the "kind of death" he hoped he might be granted.

Fragment of a Letter

January 24, 1948

... By God's grace I am slowly regaining strength. I am a servant of Rama. I will do His work so long as He wills. I shall have won if I am granted a death whereby I can demonstrate the strength of truth and non-violence. I did not display any courage in what happened on the 20th. I thought it was part of some army exercise. Had I known that it was an intimation of my death I cannot tell how I might have reacted. So I am not yet a mahatma. What does it matter if people describe me as one? I am only an ordinary mortal. Yes, if I have been sincere in my pursuit of truth, non-violence, non-stealing, brahmacharya, and so on and if I have done all this with God as my witness, I shall certainly be granted the kind of death that I seek. I have expressed the wish at the prayer meeting also that should someone kill me I may have no anger against the killer in my heart and I may die with Ramanama on my lips....

A few days later Gandhi looks back on his experience in South Africa, commenting on his part long ago in the South African struggle for Indian rights. Gandhi challenges readers with his hopes for South Africa and India.

From Speech at Prayer Meeting

New Delhi
January 28, 1948

... You know in South Africa our people are fighting for their rights. Here in India there are no laws depriving the people of the right of owning land or living wherever they please. It is true we have reduced Harijans to some such condition but for the rest of society that is not so. But I have seen with my own eyes that that is so in South Africa. The Indians therefore are having to put up a struggle ... they claim to be satyagrahis and their struggle has taken the form of satyagraha. They keep on sending cables. They cannot even move from one province to another without a permit. South Africa is like a continent. It is a very large country. Indians wishing to go to the Transvaal from Natal can do so only if they have a permit. They say it is as much their country as anyone else's and ask why there should be such restrictions imposed on their movements. Many have succeeded in moving to the Transvaal and the Government this time has been decent. They have not been arrested so far. They first went to Volksrust which is the first city after crossing the border. There were policemen present in strength but they only looked on and did not arrest them. There they found a motor vehicle and proceeded in it further on. Then a meeting was held there at which they were given a warm welcome. I thought I should give you this information. These Indians have performed an act of great courage. Indians in South Africa are few in number but, if they all become true satyagrahis, their victory is certain and no obstacle can stop them. But this has yet to be achieved. There are, as here, many kinds of people. There are Hindus and there are Muslims. They all work together. They know they cannot fight their battle separately. They have reached Johannesburg but they cannot stop there. They must go on and on till they are arrested. The Government have a right to arrest them, for satyagraha implies the acceptance of punishment for the violation of a law. They deserve congratulations. I shall ask the Government of South Africa not to be too severe with people who carry on their struggle with such decency. They should understand their grievances and come to a settlement with them. Why should it be that one with a white skin cannot have a dialogue with one with a black skin? Why should Indians have to fight for their legitimate rights? How does it harm the whites if Indians too are allowed to live there? Today we are also a free country as South Africa is and are members of the same Commonwealth, which implies that we should all live like brothers and equals. But if they consider Indians their enemies and deprive them of their basic civic rights, then they are not behaving as friends but as enemies. It is something which is difficult to understand. Why should they look down on the coloured people? Is it because they are industrious and thrifty? I shall tell the Government of South Africa through this meeting that it should mend its ways. I have myself lived in South Africa for twenty years and I can therefore say that it is my country. I should have told you all this yesterday but I could not do so. . . .

From A Talk (Gandhi's last public statement)

Wherever I go I find our plight the same as that of the Yadavas[129] who met their doom killing one another. No one realizes how much harm we are doing to society by being engaged in our personal feuds. But what can you or anyone else do about it? This indicates a failure on my part. What could anyone do when God made me blind to these things? But let me set things right as far as possible, while I am alive, so that the coming generation may not hurl abuses at me. If I succeed in it, I shall regard it as God's grace. . . .

After this talk two men wanted an appointment with Gandhi. Being busy, Gandhi said: "Tell them I shall talk with them during my walk after the prayers, if I am alive."

On the next page are the last scenes in the last act of Gandhi's life as reported by those who were with him.

129. Yadavas: an Indian clan

Remarks on Way to Prayer Meeting

New Delhi
January 30, 1948

"Bapu, your watch must be feeling neglected. You would not look at it," remarked Abha.

Why should I, since you are my time-keepers?

"But you do not look at the time-keepers," rejoined one of them. Bapu again laughed. The last remark that he uttered as he cleared the steps leading to the prayer ground was:

It is your fault that I am ten minutes late. It is the duty of nurses to carry on their work even if God himself should be present there. If it is time to give medicine to a patient and one feels hesitant about it, the poor patient will die. So it is with prayers. It irks me if I am late for prayers even by a minute.

Manu Gandhi's Account

According to Manu Gandhi's account, as Gandhiji passed along the cordoned lane through the prayer congregation, he took his hands off the shoulders of the two girls to acknowledge the namaskars[130] of the prayer congregation. All of a sudden someone from the crowd roughly elbowed his way to them. Manu Gandhi, thinking that he was coming forward to touch Gandhiji's feet, remonstrated saying something about it being already late for the prayer and tried to stop the intruder by thrusting back his hand. He violently pushed her away, causing the notebook she was carrying in her hands to fall down. As she stooped down to pick up the scattered things, he planted himself in front of Gandhi and fired in quick succession three shots at point-blank range. The last words Gandhiji uttered were "Raam, Raa … m." A spreading crimson spot on the white clothes. The hands which had been raised in namaskar to the gathering slowly came down. The limp body softly sank to the ground. Gandhi breathed his last at 5:17 p.m.

130. namaskars: gesture of greeting, sometimes accompanied by the word "Namaste" (literally "I bow to you"; sometimes translated, "I honor the place in you which is of love, of truth, of light, of peace")

Study Guide

Our world is very different from the world in which Gandhi lived. The population of the world has tripled since 1948. There were then about two billion people; there are now over six billion. National political structures have changed radically. With the break-up of empires dominated mostly by European powers, the number of independent nation-states has increased greatly. Gandhi's India itself has become three independent nations: India, Pakistan, and Bangladesh. Colonies in Asia and Africa have become nation-states. In 1950 two different economic systems, centrally planned economies and market economies, were contending for dominance. The world was, for a time, divided into a first world (capitalist), a second world (socialist or communist), and a third world (struggling and poverty-stricken). Leading nations in both the first and second world had nuclear arsenals sufficient to destroy each other. Now, centrally planned economies have, for the most part, failed, and their successors have become part—sometimes not a very effective part—of a worldwide market economy that is currently dominated by first world economies. Colonialism in the old sense has given way to a domination by the market that benefits the richer nations, while the poor—countries and individuals—struggle to survive.

Newer technologies, especially in communication, transportation, and military power, have changed the nature of the struggle that is going on. Gandhi's spinning wheel, which was never accepted except as a political symbol, is an anachronism. At the same time, rapidly developing technologies and growing populations are damaging the ecosystem in ways that may make it unrecoverable. Bigness is everywhere winning out over smallness, though there are places where a few are managing to make a living for themselves and their families in ways that Gandhi hoped would finally win out.

At the same time, religious and cultural ideologies have become more militant and more dangerous as part of the mix. Around the world, conflicts, often lethal ones, persist—Hindus vs. Muslims in the subcontinent; Muslims vs. Christians in the Balkans and Middle East; Muslims vs. Jews in Palestine; Orthodox Christians vs. Catholic Christians in Eastern Europe; and "fundamentalists" vs. "universalists" within the major religions themselves.

Gandhi's writings in this volume are primarily of three categories, although they are sometimes intertwined: non-violent political action (satyagraha); economic development (swadeshi); and religious development, with particular attention to conflicts among religions and the repressive character of some religious theory and activity. The questions below look at Gandhi's ideas and actions, in the many areas in which he worked, as they may relate to our own situation. This means understanding Gandhi and then applying him to the contemporary world. It may also mean reinterpreting Gandhi for our own time.

Questions to Consider

1. Gandhi communicated directly with leaders whom he opposed, such as Lord Irwin in 1930, Dr. Ambedkar in 1933, and Lord Linlithgow in 1940. What might Gandhi have gained through such communication? How do you evaluate his letter to Hitler in 1939, even if it was not delivered? What lessons can we take from Gandhi's use of direct communication?

2. The Salt March may have been Gandhi's greatest satyagraha campaign. What contributed to its success?

3. When Gandhi attended the London Round Table Conference, he expected little to be accomplished. How do you assess his interviews with the press, his broadcast to America, and his activities in England (such as represented in his London Diary)?

4. Why do you think Gandhi's stand against untouchability was so important to him?

5. Gandhi's practice of fasting is a complicated issue, as can be seen during his efforts to remove untouchability. How do you assess the responses by others to the fast in 1933? How well does he justify the fast? Do his motives for fasting speak to anything in your life?

6. Gandhi gained a great deal from the New Testament, particularly Jesus's Sermon on the Mount. Would you agree that Gandhi is a model for applying Jesus's teaching?

7. Gandhi never rejected Hinduism, but he sought to reform it, and he took into it a great deal from other religions, especially Christianity and Islam. Does a universalist religion (such as Gandhi's way of practicing Hinduism) make sense in our world?

8. Gandhi supported the British during World War I partly because he saw himself as a citizen of the British Empire, and partly because he did not want to take advantage of Britain during a time of crisis. Why does his perspective change during World War II?

9. Do Gandhi's ideas for Peace Brigades and a Nonviolent Volunteer Corps have potential in our violent world? How might Peace Brigades or a Nonviolent Volunteer Corps function in the world today?

10. What can we take from Gandhi's writings about violence and nonviolence? Would you call him idealistic or realistic? Are idealism and realism antithetical?

11. Given the problems of economic globalization, is there room for small scale "village industries" as Gandhi envisioned them? Might Gandhi's ideas for village-based economics become important in the future? To what extent do you agree with this statement by Vandana Shiva: "... Gandhi's idea of swadeshi—that local societies should put their own resources and capacities to use to meet their needs as a basic element of freedom—is becoming increasingly relevant. We cannot afford to forget that we need self-rule, especially in this world of globalization" (qtd. by David Barsamian, *The Progressive*, September 1997, 38)?

12. Do you agree with the following statement by Vandana Shiva that Gandhi's politics create "permanent democracy?" Is civil disobedience essential to democracy?

> My links with Gandhi now are very political links because I do not believe there is any other politics available to us in the late twentieth century, a period of a totalitarianism linked with the market. There is really no other way you can do politics and create freedom for people without the kinds of instruments he revived. Civil disobedience is a way to create permanent democracy, perennial democracy, a direct democracy. (qtd. by David Barsamian, *The Progressive*, September 1997, 38)

13. One person who has studied Gandhi's influence, Rajni Bakshi, has contrasted the ancient bazaar with Wall Street. In the bazaar, people had conversations "and buying and selling were tossed together with storytelling, politics and even the framing of moral values"; on Wall Street, a complex mechanism of indirect and distant exchange, "virtually all functions of life are seen to be best served by the pecuniary motive." She quotes the economist Jeremy Rifkin as saying, "Can civilization survive when only the commercial sphere is left as the primary mediator of human life?" (*Bazaars, Conversations & Freedom* 4-5). Would you agree that Gandhi's ideas help us imagine a healthier economics or a healthier society?

14. Gandhi established four intentional communities, two in South Africa, Phoenix and Tolstoy Farm, and two in India, Ahmedabad (later called Satyagraha Ashram) and Sevagram. (He also seems to have been greatly impressed by the Trappist monastery near Durban that he visited in 1895). Do such intentional communities have a function today? How would you feel about living in such a community?

15. During his last months, Gandhi struggled with the partition of India and Pakistan. How do you see this affecting him and his last writings?

16. We get a glimpse of how Gandhi saw God, how he handled Kasturba's death, what he believed about the afterlife in his letter to Amiya Chakravarty, and how he approached prayer. Do these writings change your image of Gandhi? What do you take away from his spiritual writings?

Sources and Influences

One who wishes to understand Gandhi's thought would do well to become familiar with writings that Gandhi himself refers to again and again. We recommend study of the *Bhagavad-Gita* (probably the most widely read of Hindu religious writings), the Sermon on the Mount, the hymns "Lead, Kindly Light" (by John Henry Newman) and "When I Survey the Wondrous Cross" (by Isaac Watts), John Ruskin's *Unto this Last*, and Tolstoy's *The Kingdom of God is Within You.*

Glossary[131]

Ahimsa: nonviolence, non-injury, non-destruction of life

Akhadas: training gyms

Ashram: a retreat or center for communal living, research and study, for followers of a particular path

Ba: Gujarati expression meaning mother; used for Gandhi's wife Kastur (Kasturba, or Kasturbai) by him and others

Bania: member of a subgroup of the third caste, the Vaishyas, comprised of businessmen, merchants, herders, and farmers. The four main castes, or varnas, are Brahmin, Kshatriya, Vaishya, and Shudra. Below the four varnas are untouchables, also known as Harijans or Dalits.

Bapu: "Father"; term of affection used for Gandhi by many Indians, not just his wife and sons

Basala: a carpenter's tool

Bhajans: devotional songs

Brahmacharya: celibacy; chastity in quest for God; used by Gandhi to mean control not only of the sexual appetite but control of all the senses, hence freedom from desire and lust

Brahman: the ultimate reality, the Supreme Being

Brahmin: member of the highest caste sanctioned by Hinduism; literally one who knows Brahman, the Supreme Being

Chapattis (chapatis): flatbread

Charkha: spinning wheel

Crore: 10 million

Dacoits: bandits

Dalit: suppressed or down-trodden; belonging to an "untouchable" group; the term that is politically preferred

Darshan: blessing obtained by being in the presence of someone or something revered; showing respect by touching of the feet of an elder or a guru

Daya: mercy, compassion

131. Sources for this Glossary include Joan Bondurant's *Conquest of Violence*; Narayan Desai's *The Fire and the Rose*; Rajmohan Gandhi's *Gandhi: The Man, His People, and the Empire*; Anthony J. Parel's edition of Gandhi's *Hind Swaraj;* and Kathryn Tidrick's *Gandhi: A Political and Spiritual Life.*

Dharma: generally, the righteous performance of duty; right course of conduct or action; natural moral law; religion as ethics and religion as sect

Dhurna (dharna, dharana): a form of sit-down strike

Dhoti: loincloth; loose lower garment for males

Diwali: festival of lights and the renewal of life

Dumb: voiceless, speechless—should not be interpreted as referring to a lack of intelligence

Gajendra moksha bhajan: section of the Gita telling of an elephant king

Gandhiji: "ji" is added after names as an expression of reverence and respect

Ghee: clarified butter

Goondas: thugs

Gujaratis: members of the state of Gujarat where Gandhi was born and grew up

Harijan: term popularized by Gandhi for an "untouchable"; literally, "child of God"; a member of the lowest group in Indian society; see Dalit; also, the title of the English-language periodical Gandhi edited, beginning in 1933

Hartal: voluntary closing of shops and suspension of work as a form of protest; also, as a sign of mourning

He Govinda rakho sharan: a Hindu devotional hymn

Himsa: violence or envy

Kalma: Islamic prayer beginning "there is no God but Allah"

Karma: literally, action; the law of retribution by which one's past actions determine one's future fate

Khadi (khaddar): handspun and hand-woven cloth, made famous by Gandhi

Koran Sharif: the holy Koran (Quran)

Kottis: cottages or homes

Kum-Kum: red powder (usually turmeric or saffron)

Lakh: 100,000

Mahatma: great soul

Majlis: the parliament

Mantra: sound or word used to focus meditation

Mohalla: neighborhood

Muslim League: the political group, founded in 1906, which at first worked for Hindu-Muslim unity, but later called for a separate Muslim nation, leading to the partition of India and Pakistan
Mussalman: archaic for Muslim
Namaskars: gesture of greeting, sometimes accompanied by the word "Namaste" (literally "I bow to you"; sometimes translated, among other phrases, "I honor the place in you which is of love, of truth, of light, of peace")
***Navajivan*:** the weekly periodical in Gujarati, also in English as *Young India*, which Gandhi began publishing in 1919
Panchayat: village council, with customary legal authority
Pandit: one who has memorized large portions of the Vedas, usually a Brahmin; origin of the English "pundit"
Pice: a very small coin (the modern rupee is divided into 100 pice)
Plinth: a square block serving as a base
Praja: Gandhi's term for "nation" in *Hind Swaraj*
Purna Swaraj: full independence
"Raam, Raa ... m": "O God"; thought to be Gandhi's last words upon being shot
The Raj: the British regime in India
Ramadhun: devotional song of lord Rama
Ramanama: the chanting of the name Ram, the hero of the Ramayana
Rupees (Rs.): the common currency of India
Ryots: peasants or tenant farmers
Sadhus: holy men
Samadhis: those who have achieved the level of spiritual concentration just short of nirvana
Sanatanist: a sect which believed in preserving traditional forms of Hindu practice
Sannyasis: monks, hermits, ascetics
Sardar: political leader or commander
Satya: truth
Satyagraha: literally, firmness for the truth; truth-force, usually translated as "nonviolent resistance"; the technique developed by Gandhi for social and political change, based on truth, nonviolence, and self-suffering
Satyagrahi: one who practices satyagraha

Shanti dals: peace brigades
Shastras: religious treatises
Shloka: prayer, song, stanza
Swadeshi: belonging to, of, or made in one's own country
Swaraj: "self-rule"; used by Indian nationalists to denote independence from Britain (purna swaraj denoted full independence); used by Gandhi to mean political and economic independence, as well as self-discipline
Tapasya: self-discipline, religious penance; sacrifice; austerity
Untouchable: a member of the subclasses excluded from and considered ritually unclean and defiling by the four Hindu classes
Vikram Samvat: popular Hindu lunar calendar
Yadavas: an Indian clan
Yajna: ritual
Zamindars: landlords

Citations

Listed below for each selection are the volume and page(s) in *The Collected Works of Mahatma Gandhi-CD* or the volume, issue, and page(s) in *Harijan*. Dates below are given as day.month.year. When two dates were provided in the source, such as when a speech was delivered and when it was published, the earlier date is listed here. Approximate dates are indicated by brackets.

Contents	**Date**	***CWMG-CD* or *Harijan***
Chapter 1 Salt March and London Round Table (1930–1931)		
The Salt March (1930)		
Letter to Lord Irwin	2.3.30	48:362-67
Speech at Prayer Meeting, Sabarmati Ashram	[12.3.30]	48:416-17
Parting Message at Chandola	12.3.30	48:417
Speech at Broach	26.3.30	48:477-80
Message to the Nation	9.4.30	49:52
Arrest at Midnight	5.5.30	49:270
Interview to The Daily Telegraph	5.5.30	49:271
Letter to E.E. Doyle	10.5.30	49:273
For the Dandi Pilgrims	14.5.31	52:100
The London Round Table Conference (1931)		
Speech at Friends House, London	12.9.31	53:348-49
Interview to the Press	12.9.31	53:350-51
Broadcast to America	13.9.31	53:353-56
Opening Speech to the Round Table Conference	15.9.31	53:364-65
Speech at Conference of Missionary Societies	8.10.31	53:468-70
Speech at Birmingham Meeting	18.10.31	54:43-48
Interview with Callender	[16.10.31]	54:21-24
Farewell Speech to the Round Table Conference	1.12.31	54:219-31
Excerpts from London Diary	14.10.31 - 30.12.31	54:332-41
Gandhi/Viceroy Telegrams	31.12.31	54:330

Chapter 2: A New Journal, A New Cause, a New Ashram (1931–1936)

To the Reader (The First Issue of *Harijan*)	11.2.33	59.232-33
Fasting for the Removal of Untouchability		
Dr. Ambedkar and Caste	11.2.33	59: 227-29
His Will Be Done	6.5.33	61:85-88
Statement Explaining Object of Fast	8.5.33	61:122-23
Comments on the Fast		
From General Smuts	6.5.33	61:87-88
From Rabindranath Tagore	11.5.33	Harijan 1:21:8
From Romain Rolland ("The Meaning of the Fast")	27.5.33	Harijan 1:16:1
From S. K. George ("Is Satyagraha Christian?")	27.5.33	Harijan 1:16:5-6
All About the Fast	8.7.33	61:219-22
A "Double Hell"	1.11.33	62:243-44
Statement to the Press ("Shall It Be On Foot?")	11.5.34	63:471-72
Duty of Bread Labour	29.6.35	67:207-08
A Discussion with Maurice Frydman	[25.8.35]	69:320-21
The Greatest Force	12.10.35	68:56-59
Talk with Kumarappa	[2.9.36]	69:336-37
On My Recent Illness	19.9.36	69:375-77
Excerpt from Speech at Gujarati Sahitya Parishad	31.10.36	70:31-35

Chapter 3: World War II in Europe (1938–1945)

Before the Outbreak of War		
Qualifications of a Peace Brigade	18.6.38	73:243-45
If I Were a Czech	6.10.38	74:90-92
Logical Consequence	8.10.38	74:98-100
Letter to Adolf Hitler	23.7.39	76:156-57
After the Outbreak of War		
Statement to the Press	5.9.39	76:311-12

Statement to "The New Chronicle"	4.12.39	71:6-7 (bound vol)
Statement to the Press	6.2.1940	77:300-03
Statement to The Daily Herald	7.2.1940	77:306-07
My Position	9.4.1940	78:132
How to Combat Hitlerism	18.6.40	78:343-45
Political Involvement		
My Idea of a Police Force	20.8.40	79:137-38
Equal Distribution	19.8.40	79:133-35
from Viceroy-Gandhi Correspondence	30.9.40	79:474-75, 275-77
Civil Disobedience	15.10.40	79:306-10
Why Suspension	24.10.40	79:328-329
Expansion of the War		
Discussion at Working Committee	[30.12.41]	81:396-97
The Ashram Prayer	2.2.42	81:487-89
Plea for Calmness	17.2.42	82:28-29
Nonviolent Resistance	5.4.42	82:167-69
To American Friends	3.8.42	83:162-64
Mahatmaji's Arrest	16.8.42	Harijan 9:31:273
Request to Government on Kasturba's Funeral	22.2.44	84:17
Discussion with D. Ramaswami	[3.8.44]	84:265-66

Chapter 4: Postwar Reconstruction (1946–1947)

What Ought to be Done	14.2.46	89:395-96
Gandhiji on New Spirit	[17.3.46]	90:99-100
Non-Violent Volunteer Corps	26.4.46	90:314-16
Independence	29.4.46	90:327-28
Press Summary of Churchill's Speech	29.4.46	90:432-33
How Can Violence Be Stopped?	9.5.46	90:373-74
Religion v No Religion	29.5.46	91:61-62
Is God a Person or a Principle?	8.8.46	91:427-28
Alternative to Industrialism	28.8.46	92:63-64

Shrirampur Diary	2.12.46	Harijan 10:48:479
Letter from Gandhiji	5.12.46	Harijan 10:48:476
The "Do or Die" Mission	8.12.46	Harijan 10:44:432

Chapter 5: Last Months (1947-1948)

Personal Writings

Letter to Amiya Chakravarty	11.8.47	96:210
Letter to Lord Mountbatten	30.8.47	96:303
Note on Gandhiji's 78th Birthday	10.47	97:474-75
Letter to Lord Mountbatten	9.11.47	97:265
Speech at Prayer Meeting	12.11.47	97: 297-98
A Note (To a Member of the All India Village Industries Association)	17.11.47	97:339
A Talk	5.12.47	97:472

Last Fast and Death

Question Box	10.12.47	98:21-22
Talk with a Sikh Friend	13.1.48	98:223
Gandhi's Talk to Prayer Meeting	13.1.48	98:227
Letter to Gujaratis	14.1.48	98:229
Speech from Bed	15.1.48	98:236
Letter to Mira	16.1.48	98:240
Speech at Prayer Meeting	16.1.48	98:244-45
Speech at Prayer Meeting	17.1.48	98:248
Speech before Breaking Fast	18.1.48	98:254-57
Fragment of a Letter	24.1.48	98:297-98
Speech at Prayer Meeting	28.1.48	98:323-24
Last Public Statement	30.1.48	98:339
Remarks on Way to Prayer Meeting	30.1.48	98:341
Manu Gandhi's Account of the Assassination		98:341n3

Bibliography

Encyclopedias and most online references are not listed below but are cited in footnotes in the text.

Gandhi Primary Sources:

Gandhi, Mohandas K. *Autobiography: The Story of My Experiments with Truth.* 1927, 1929. New York: Dover, 1983.

———. *The Collected Works of Mahatma Gandhi.* 100 vols. Delhi: Publications Division, Ministry of Information and Broadcasting, Govt. of India, 1958.

———. *The Collected Works of Mahatma Gandhi-CD.* Ministry of Information and Broadcasting, Govt. of India, 1999.

———. *Hind Swaraj or Indian Home Rule.* Ed. Anthony J. Parel. 1910. London: Cambridge UP, 1997.

———. Selections from newspapers, which Gandhi published: *Indian Opinion*, *Young India*, *Navjivan*, and *Harijan*.

Gandhi's Life and Thought:

Alexander, Horace. *Gandhi Through Western Eyes.* 1969. Philadelphia: New Society, 1984.

Bakshi, Rajni. Bapu Kuti: J*ourneys in Rediscovery of Gandhi.* New Delhi: Penguin, 1998.

———. Bazaars, *Conversations & Freedom: For a Market Culture Beyond Greed and Fear.* New Delhi: Penguin Books, 2009.

Bondurant, Joan V. *Conquest of Violence: The Gandhian Philosophy of Conflict.* U of California P, 1969.

Brown, Judith M. *Gandhi: Prisoner of Hope.* London: Yale UP, 1989.

Chadha, Yogesh. *Gandhi: A Life.* New York: John Wiley, 1997.

Cortright, David. *Gandhi and Beyond: Nonviolence for a New PoliticalAge.* 2nd edition. Boulder, CO: Paradigm, 2009.

Dalton, Dennis Gilmore. *Mahatma Gandhi: Nonviolent Power in Action.* New York: Columbia UP, 1993.

Desai, Narayan. *The Fire and the Rose.* Trans. Chitra Desai. Ahmedabad: *Navajivan*, 1995.

Diwan, Romesh, and Mark Lutz. *Essays on Gandhian Economics.* Gandhi Peace Foundation, 1985.

Easwaran, Eknath. *Nonviolent Soldier of Islam: Badshah Khan, A Man to Match His Mountains.* Tomales, CA: Nilgiri P, 1999.

Erikson, Erik H. *Gandhi's Truth: On the Origins of Militant Nonviolence.* New York: Norton, 1969.

Fischer, Louis. *Gandhi: His Life and Message for the World.* 1965. New York: New American Library, 1982.

Gandhi, Arun, and Sunanda Gandhi. *The Forgotten Woman: The Untold Story of Kastur Gandhi, Wife of Mahatma Gandhi.* Huntsville, AR: Ozark Mountain Publishers, 1998.

Gandhi, Rajmohan. *Gandhi: The Man, His People, and the Empire.* Berkeley: University of California P, 2007.

Green, Martin B. Gandhi: *Voice of a New Age Revolution.* New York: Continuum, 1993.

Hardiman, David. *Gandhi in His Time and Ours: The Global Legacy of His Ideas.* Columbia UP, 2003.

Harris, Ishwar C. *Gandhians in Contemporary India: The Vision and the Visionaries.* Mellon P, 1999.

Hick, John, and Lamont C. Hempel. *Gandhi's Significance for Today.* New York: St. Martin's, 1989.

Hunt, James D. *Gandhi in London.* 1978. Revised ed. Springfield, VA: Nataraj Books, 1993.

Ingram, Catherine. *In the Footsteps of Gandhi: Conversations with Spiritual Social Activists.* Berkeley, CA: Parallax, 2003.

Jordens, J. T. F. *Gandhi's Religion: A Homespun Shawl.* New York: St. Martin's, 1998.

Juergensmeyer, Mark. *Gandhi's Way: A Handbook on Conflict Resolution.* 1984. Berkeley: U of California P, 2002.

Mani Bhavan Gandhi Sangrahalaya: Mahatma Gandhi Information Website. www.gandhi-manibhavan.org

M.K. Gandhi Institute for Nonviolence, web site: www.gandhiinstitute.org.

Muzumdar, Haridas T., and Will Durant. *Gandhi versus the Empire.* New York: Manhattan P, 1932.

Nayar, Sushila. *Kasturba: Wife of Gandhi.* Wallingford, PA: Pendle Hill, 1948.

Parekh, Bhikhu. *Gandhi.* Oxford, UK: Oxford UP, 1997.

Payne, Robert. *The Life and Death of Mahatma Gandhi.* New York: Smithmark, 1969.

Shepard, Mark. *Gandhi Today: The Story of Mahatma Gandhi's Successors.* Washington, DC: Seven Locks, 1987.

Shirer, William L. *Gandhi: A Memoir.* New Delhi: Rupa, 1993.

Tidrick, Kathryn. *Gandhi: A Political and Spiritual Life.* London: I.B. Tauris, 2006.

Wolpert, Stanley. *Gandhi's Passion: The Life and Legacy of Mahatma Gandhi.* Oxford: Oxford UP, 2001

Index of Persons

Editor Biographical Information

Sterling Olmsted first encountered India when, as a teenager, he purchased a used copy of the *Bhagavad-Gita*. It was more than 40 years before he made his first trip to India. Born in 1915, Sterling taught English for 29 years at Rensselaer Polytechnic Institute and then was a professor and provost at Wilmington College in Ohio from 1968 to 1995. He is a member of Campus Friends Meeting (OH), sojourning at Schenectady Friends Meeting (NY). His first Nonviolence and Social Change course at Wilmington College focused on Woolman and Gandhi.

Mike Heller teaches literature, writing, and Peace and Justice Studies at Roanoke College. He has edited *The Tendering Presence: Essays on John Woolman* and written "From West Point to Quakerism" (both Pendle Hill Publications) as well as articles on the personal journal, autobiography, and the place of spirituality in education. He is a member of the Roanoke Friends Meeting (VA). He and Sterling Olmsted co-edited *John Woolman: A Nonviolence and Social Change Source Book* (Wilmington College Peace Resource Center).

Ruth Olmsted is Sterling's daughter. A lifelong academic, she taught humanities courses at colleges in Ohio, Iowa, and New York for 20 years before coming to Excelsior College (then called Regents College) in 1993 to oversee the development of its college-level proficiency exam series. She came late to the Gandhi project, serving as more of a managing editor to polish the final manuscript after her father and Mike Heller had selected the excerpts and created the structure. She is a member of Schenectady Friends Meeting (NY).

CPSIA information can be obtained at www.ICGtesting.com
Printed in the USA
LVOW120256211112

308291LV00008B/5/P

9 780965 886642